Apples in Slaw: 91 Delicious Recipes for Coleslaw Lovers

The Crepe Corner Tsuz

Copyright © 2023 The Crepe Corner Tsuz
All rights reserved.
:

Contents

INTRODUCTION 7
1. Classic Apple Coleslaw 9
2. BBQ Apple Coleslaw 9
3. Spicy Apple Coleslaw 10
4. Creamy Apple Coleslaw 11
5. Tangy Apple Coleslaw 12
6. Sweet Apple Coleslaw 13
7. Greek Apple Coleslaw 14
8. Indian Apple Coleslaw 15
9. Thai Apple Coleslaw 16
10. Mexican Apple Coleslaw 16
11. Caribbean Apple Coleslaw 17
12. German Apple Coleslaw 18
13. Italian Apple Coleslaw 19
14. French Apple Coleslaw 20
15. Japanese Apple Coleslaw 21
16. Korean Apple Coleslaw 22
17. Vietnamese Apple Coleslaw 23
18. Chinese Apple Coleslaw 23
19. Moroccan Apple Coleslaw 24
20. Lebanese Apple Coleslaw 25
21. Egyptian Apple Coleslaw 26
22. Israeli Apple Coleslaw 27
23. Irish Apple Coleslaw 28
24. Scottish Apple Coleslaw 29
25. Welsh Apple Coleslaw 29
26. English Apple Coleslaw 30
27. Dutch Apple Coleslaw 31

28. Belgian Apple Coleslaw 32

29. Swedish Apple Coleslaw 33

30. Norwegian Apple Coleslaw 34

31. Danish Apple Coleslaw 35

32. Finnish Apple Coleslaw 36

33. Estonian Apple Coleslaw 36

34. Latvian Apple Coleslaw 37

35. Lithuanian Apple Coleslaw 38

36. Polish Apple Coleslaw 39

37. Russian Apple Coleslaw 40

38. Ukrainian Apple Coleslaw 41

39. Hungarian Apple Coleslaw 42

40. Romanian Apple Coleslaw 42

41. Bulgarian Apple Coleslaw 43

42. Serbian Apple Coleslaw 44

43. Croatian Apple Coleslaw 45

44. Slovenian Apple Coleslaw 46

45. Bosnian Apple Coleslaw 46

46. Albanian Apple Coleslaw 47

47. Greek-style Apple Coleslaw with Feta 48

48. Chicken and Apple Coleslaw 49

49. Turkey and Apple Coleslaw 50

50. Pork and Apple Coleslaw 51

51. Beef and Apple Coleslaw 52

52. Fish and Apple Coleslaw 53

53. Shrimp and Apple Coleslaw 54

54. Crab and Apple Coleslaw 54

55. Lobster and Apple Coleslaw 55

56. Scallop and Apple Coleslaw 56

57. Tuna and Apple Coleslaw 57

58. Salmon and Apple Coleslaw 58

59. Trout and Apple Coleslaw 59

60. Halibut and Apple Coleslaw 60

61. Cod and Apple Coleslaw 61

62. Haddock and Apple Coleslaw 62

63. Flounder and Apple Coleslaw 63

64. Sole and Apple Coleslaw 63

65. Tilapia and Apple Coleslaw 64

66. Catfish and Apple Coleslaw 65

67. Mahi Mahi and Apple Coleslaw 66

68. Red Snapper and Apple Coleslaw 67

69. Grouper and Apple Coleslaw 68

70. Swordfish and Apple Coleslaw 69

71. Vegetable Apple Coleslaw 70

72. Fruit Apple Coleslaw 71

73. Nut and Apple Coleslaw 72

74. Seed Apple Coleslaw 73

75. Cheese Apple Coleslaw 74

76. Avocado and Apple Coleslaw 75

77. Egg and Apple Coleslaw 76

78. Bacon and Apple Coleslaw 76

79. Ham and Apple Coleslaw 77

80. Sausage and Apple Coleslaw 78

81. Pepperoni and Apple Coleslaw 79

82. Mushroom and Apple Coleslaw 80

83. Onion and Apple Coleslaw 81

84. Garlic and Apple Coleslaw 81

85. Tomato and Apple Coleslaw 83

86. Cucumber and Apple Coleslaw 83
87. Carrot and Apple Coleslaw 84
88. Beet and Apple Coleslaw 85
89. Parsnip and Apple Coleslaw 86
90. Yam and Apple Coleslaw 87
91. Sweet Potato and Apple Coleslaw 88
CONCLUSION 89

INTRODUCTION

Apples are a versatile ingredient that can be eaten as a snack, cooked into a savory dish, or incorporated into a sweet treat. But have you ever considered using apples in coleslaw? This cookbook is your guide to unlocking the delicious potential of apples in slaw.

Coleslaw is a staple side dish that can be found at practically any barbecue, potluck, or family gathering. But often, coleslaw can be bland and uninspiring. By adding apples to the mix, you can elevate the flavor profile of coleslaw and create a dish that stands out from the rest.

With 91 delicious recipes, this cookbook is a must-have for coleslaw lovers of all kinds. Whether you prefer traditional coleslaw with a twist or something completely wild and wacky, there's a recipe for everyone in this book.

Some of the recipes you'll find within the pages of Apples in Slaw include classic coleslaw with apples, spicy apple slaw, apple and bacon coleslaw, apple and cabbage slaw with toasted walnuts, and even an apple and cinnamon dessert coleslaw. Each recipe is easy to follow and includes a list of ingredients that can be found at any grocery store.

The beauty of coleslaw is that it's a customizable dish, and the addition of apples only makes it easier to customize to your liking. Whether you prefer a tangy coleslaw or something with a little more sweetness, apples provide a versatile flavor that can cater to any taste.

With so many different varieties of apples, there's no shortage of options when it comes to experimenting with this ingredient in your coleslaw. From sweet and juicy Honeycrisp apples to tangy Granny Smiths, there's a type of apple that will work perfectly with any coleslaw recipe.

Apples not only bring a delicious flavor to coleslaw but also provide a variety of health benefits. Apples are low in calories, high in fiber, and packed with essential vitamins and minerals. By incorporating apples into your coleslaw, you're not only adding flavor but also boosting the nutritional value of the dish.

Overall, Apples in Slaw is a cookbook that every coleslaw lover should have in their collection. With 91 unique and flavorful recipes, this book will inspire you to try new things and create a coleslaw that's truly your own. Whether you're hosting a summer barbecue or bringing a side dish to a potluck, your coleslaw will be the talk of the party with the help of this cookbook.

1. Classic Apple Coleslaw

This classic apple coleslaw recipe is perfect for a BBQ or family dinner. It combines the crunchy texture of cabbage and the sweetness of apples to make a tasty and refreshingly balanced side dish.
Serving: 4
Preparation time: 10 minutes
Ready time: 10 minutes

Ingredients:
- 4 cups shredded cabbage
- 1 large onion, finely chopped
- 1 tart apple, finely chopped
- 1/2 cup mayonnaise
- 2 tbsp apple cider vinegar
- 1/4 cup golden raisins
- Salt & pepper to taste

Instructions:
1. In a large bowl, combine cabbage, onion, and apple.
2. In a small bowl, whisk together mayonnaise, apple cider vinegar, salt and pepper.
3. Pour dressing over cabbage mixture, mixing to coat evenly.
4. Add raisins and mix to combine.
5. Serve immediately or chill until ready to serve.

Nutrition Information: Serving Size: 1/4 of recipe; Calories: 155, Total Fat: 10.6g, Cholesterol: 15mg, Sodium: 158mg, Total Carbohydrates: 14.3g, Sugar: 9.3g, Protein: 2g.

2. BBQ Apple Coleslaw

BBQ Apple Coleslaw is an easy and delicious side-dish filled with BBQ sauce, apples, and crunchy coleslaw mix. Perfect for a summer BBQ or potluck, this dish is sure to leave you wanting more!
Serving: 4-6
Preparation Time: 10 minutes

Ready Time: 30 minutes

Ingredients:
- 2 cups coleslaw mix
- 1 apple, diced
- 1/2 cup BBQ sauce
- 1 tablespoon brown sugar
- 1 tablespoon white distilled vinegar
- 2 teaspoons Dijon mustard
- Salt and pepper, to taste

Instructions:
1. In a bowl, mix together the coleslaw mix and diced apple.
2. In a separate smaller bowl, mix together the BBQ sauce, brown sugar, white distilled vinegar, and Dijon mustard. Add salt and pepper, to taste.
3. Pour the BBQ and sugar mixture over the coleslaw and apple mixture, and mix until everything is coated.
4. Refrigerate for at least 30 minutes before serving.

Nutrition Information (per serving):
Calories: 170; Fat: 4 g; Carbohydrates: 32 g; Protein: 3 g

3. Spicy Apple Coleslaw

This flavorful and crunchy Spicy Apple Coleslaw is the perfect accompaniment to any dish. It's easy to make and features a delicious combination of apples, carrots, and cabbage in a creamy, spicy sauce.
Serving: 6 servings
Preparation time: 10 minutes
Ready time: 15 minutes

Ingredients:
- 2 cups shredded cabbage
- 2 cups shredded carrots
- 1 cup apple, diced
- ⅓ cup mayonnaise
- 1 tablespoon honey
- 2 teaspoons Dijon mustard

- 2 tablespoons apple cider vinegar
- 1 teaspoon hot sauce
- 1 teaspoon garlic powder
- Salt and pepper to taste

Instructions:
1. In a large bowl, combine the cabbage, carrots, and apple.
2. In a separate bowl, whisk together the mayonnaise, honey, Dijon mustard, vinegar, hot sauce, garlic powder, salt, and pepper.
3. Pour the sauce over the vegetables in the large bowl and mix to combine.
4. Chill for at least 15 minutes before serving.

Nutrition Information:
Calories: 145
Fat: 9.9g
Carbohydrates: 14.3g
Protein: 1.7g

4. Creamy Apple Coleslaw

Creamy Apple Coleslaw
Serving: 4-6
Preparation Time: 10 minutes
Ready Time: 15 minutes

Ingredients:
2 cups cabbage, shredded
1 cup red apple, thinly sliced
1/3 cup carrots, shredded
1/4 cup mayonnaise
2 tsp white sugar
1/2 tsp white vinegar
1 tsp poppy seeds

Instructions:
1. In a large bowl, combine shredded cabbage, thinly sliced red apple, and shredded carrots.

2. In a separate bowl, mix together mayonnaise, white sugar, white vinegar, and poppy seeds.
3. Pour the mayonnaise mixture over the cabbage mixture and toss to coat.
4. Refrigerate for at least 15 minutes to allow the flavors to combine.

Nutrition Information:
Calories: 104 kcal; Carbohydrates: 9.9 g; Protein: 0.7 g; Fat: 7.3 g; Sodium: 60 mg; Potassium: 85 mg; Fiber: 1.6 g; Sugar: 7.8 g; Vitamin A: 1495 IU; Vitamin C: 18.1 mg; Calcium: 22 mg; Iron: 0.4 mg

5. Tangy Apple Coleslaw

Tangy Apple Coleslaw is a simple yet delightful twist on the classic coleslaw. Packed full of flavor, this dish is sure to be a hit!
Serving: 4-6
Preparation Time: 15 minutes
Ready Time: 4-6 hours

Ingredients:
- 1 head of cabbage, shredded
- 2 green apples, chopped
- 4 celery stalks, chopped
- 1/4 cup freshly squeezed lemon juice
- 1/4 cup mayonnaise
- 2 tablespoons Dijon mustard
- 2 tablespoons honey
- 1/2 teaspoon celery seed
- Salt & pepper to taste

Instructions:
1. In a large bowl, combine the cabbage, apples, and celery.
2. In a separate bowl, whisk together the mayonnaise, Dijon mustard, lemon juice, honey, celery seed, salt and pepper.
3. Pour the dressing over the cabbage mixture. Toss to evenly coat.
4. Cover the bowl and place it in the refrigerator for 4-6 hours.
5. Serve chilled.

Nutrition Information (per serving): Calories 119, Total Fat 7 g, Saturated Fat 1 g, Cholesterol 4 mg, Sodium 433 mg, Total Carbohydrate 13 g, Dietary Fiber 3 g, Sugars 8 g, Protein 2 g

6. Sweet Apple Coleslaw

Sweet Apple Coleslaw
This light, crunchy, and sweet apple coleslaw is the perfect side dish to bring to any summer potluck or barbecue. The mix of apples, cabbage, and carrots is tossed in a slightly sweet mayo and sour cream dressing.
Serving: 6-8
Preparation Time: 10 minutes
Ready Time: 10 minutes

Ingredients:
- 2 cups cabbage, shredded
- 2 apples, cored and cut into cubes
- 1 large carrot, chopped
- 1/2 cup mayonnaise
- 1/4 cup sour cream
- 2 tablespoons sugar
- 1 tablespoon white vinegar
- Salt and pepper, to taste

Instructions:
1. In a large bowl, combine the cabbage, apples, and carrots.
2. In a medium bowl, whisk together the mayonnaise, sour cream, sugar, and vinegar.
3. Pour the dressing over the cabbage mixture and toss to combine.
4. Season with salt and pepper, to taste.

Nutrition Information:
- Calories: 139 kcal
- Carbohydrates: 14 g
- Protein: 1 g
- Fat: 9 g
- Saturated Fat: 1.5 g
- Cholesterol: 4 mg

- Sodium: 175 mg
- Potassium: 155 mg
- Fiber: 2 g
- Sugar: 9 g
- Vitamin A: 2120 IU
- Vitamin C: 23.3 mg
- Calcium: 29 mg
- Iron: 0.5 mg

7. Greek Apple Coleslaw

This zesty Greek Apple Coleslaw is a delicious twist on the classic coleslaw. The sweet apples, crunchy cabbage, and a tangy Greek yogurt dressing combine to make a flavorful, healthy side dish.
Serving: 4
Preparation time: 10 mins
Ready time: 10 mins

Ingredients:
- 2 apples, diced
- 1/4 head of cabbage, shredded
- 1/4 cup toasted walnuts, chopped
- 1/4 cup red onion, diced
- 2 tablespoons olive oil
- 2 tablespoons lemon juice
- 2 tablespoons Greek yogurt
- Salt and pepper, to taste

Instructions:
1. In a large bowl, combine the diced apples, shredded cabbage, toasted walnuts, and red onion.
2. In a small bowl, combine the olive oil, lemon juice, yogurt, salt, and pepper.
3. Pour the dressing over the slaw and mix together until evenly coated.
4. Chill in the refrigerator until ready to serve.

Nutrition Information:

Calories: 135; Total Fat: 8.3g; Cholesterol: 2.3mg; Sodium: 57.6mg; Total Carbohydrates: 14.3g; Fiber: 3.8g; Sugar: 9.5g; Protein: 2.7g

8. Indian Apple Coleslaw

Indian Apple Coleslaw: This Indian-inspired creamy apple coleslaw is a perfect side dish or snack! The vibrant crunch of fresh apples and carrots pairs deliciously with a creamy blend of yogurt, mustard, and coriander. With minimal preparation time and effort required, this yummy salad can be ready in under 15 minutes.
Serving: 4
Preparation time: 10 minutes
Ready time: 15 minutes

Ingredients:
- 2 cups finely shredded cabbage
- 2 cups shredded apples
- 1 cup grated carrots
- 1/4 cup plain yogurt
- 1 tablespoon yellow mustard
- 1 teaspoon ground coriander
- Salt and pepper to taste

Instructions:
1. In a large bowl, combine the cabbage, apples, and carrots.
2. In a separate bowl, mix together the yogurt, mustard, and coriander until fully blended.
3. Pour the yogurt mixture into the bowl of cabbage and apples, and mix until all Ingredients are combined.
4. Add salt and pepper as desired.

Nutrition Information:
Serving size: 1/4 of recipe (175g)
Calories: 83kcal
Total Fat: 0.6g
Total Carbohydrates: 18.5g
Protein: 2.9g
Sodium: 154mg

Fiber: 3.4g

9. Thai Apple Coleslaw

Thai Apple Coleslaw is a refreshing and zesty twist on a classic summer salad. Its sweet and tart flavor and crunchy texture make it the perfect side dish.
Serving: 2-4
Preparation Time: 15 minutes
Ready Time: 15 minutes

Ingredients:
-3 apples (Granny Smith, Honeycrisp, or Braeburn)
-3 cups shredded cabbage
-1/4 cup lime juice
-2 tablespoons honey
-2 tablespoons fish sauce
-2 tablespoons chopped fresh cilantro
-1 teaspoon sesame oil
-1 tablespoon sesame seeds
-Salt and pepper, to taste

Instructions:
1. Peel, core and shred the apples.
2. In a large bowl, combine apples, cabbage, lime juice, honey, fish sauce, cilantro, sesame oil, sesame seeds, salt and pepper.
3. Stir everything together until all Ingredients are thoroughly combined.
4. Top with additional cilantro, sesame seeds and salt and pepper, if desired.

Nutrition Information:
Calories: 103 kcal, Carbohydrates: 22 g, Protein: 2 g, Fat: 2 g, Saturated Fat: 1 g, Sodium: 689 mg, Potassium: 224 mg, Fiber: 3 g, Sugar: 15 g, Vitamin A: 597 IU, Vitamin C: 22 mg, Calcium: 38 mg, Iron: 1 mg

10. Mexican Apple Coleslaw

Mexican Apple Coleslaw is a delicious and easy-to-make salad that will liven up any meal. It has a sweet and crunchy blend of apples, cabbage, and cilantro and is topped with a tangy dressing.
Serving: About 4 servings
Preparation time: 10 mins
Ready time: 30 mins

Ingredients:
- 2 cups shredded cabbage
- 1 apple, peeled, cored and diced
- 1/4 cup chopped fresh cilantro
- 1/4 cup mayonnaise
- 2 tablespoons apple cider vinegar
- 2 tablespoons honey
- 1 tablespoon lime juice
- Salt and pepper, to taste

Instructions:
1. In a medium bowl, mix together the shredded cabbage, diced apple, and cilantro.
2. In a separate small bowl, whisk together the mayonnaise, apple cider vinegar, honey and lime juice.
3. Pour the dressing into the cabbage mixture and stir until everything is coated.
4. Season with salt and pepper as desired.
5. Let the coleslaw chill for at least 30 minutes before serving.

Nutrition Information:
Per serving: 166 calories, 14.3 g fat, 5.2 g saturated fat, 10.5 g carbohydrates, 2.8 g protein, 1.6 g fiber, 147 mg sodium.

11. Caribbean Apple Coleslaw

Caribbean Apple Coleslaw is an easy and flavorful coleslaw with apples, cabbage, and a creamy Caribbean dressing. This fresh and fruity side dish will spice up any meal!
Serving: 6
Preparation Time: 15 minutes

Ready Time: 15 minutes

Ingredients:
- 2 cups of shredded cabbage
- 1/2 cup of Granny Smith apples, diced
- 1/2 cup of coconut, shredded
- 1/3 cup of mayonnaise
- 2 tablespoons of lime juice
- 1 tablespoon of honey
- 1 tablespoon of prepared yellow mustard
- 1 teaspoon of Caribbean seasoning mix
- 1/2 teaspoon of red pepper flakes (optional)
- Salt and freshly ground black pepper, to taste

Instructions:
1. In a large bowl, combine cabbage, apples, and coconut; set aside.
2. To a mixing bowl, add mayonnaise, lime juice, honey, prepared yellow mustard, Caribbean seasoning mix, and red pepper flakes (optional); season with salt and black pepper, to taste.
3. Whisk together until all Ingredients are well combined.
4. Pour dressing over the cabbage mixture and toss until evenly coated.
5. Serve immediately or refrigerate for 20 minutes to allow the flavors to meld before serving.

Nutrition Information:
Calories: 108 kcal, Carbohydrates: 6 g, Protein: 1 g, Fat: 9 g, Saturated Fat: 2 g, Cholesterol: 4 mg, Sodium: 195 mg, Potassium: 82 mg, Fiber: 1 g, Sugar: 3 g, Vitamin A: 159 IU, Vitamin C: 16 mg, Calcium: 22 mg, Iron: 1 mg.

12. German Apple Coleslaw

German Apple Coleslaw
Serving: 4-6
Preparation Time: 10-15 minutes
Ready Time: 20 minutes

Ingredients:

- 2 Granny Smith apples, julienned
- 1/2 cup finely sliced red onion
- 4 oz cabbage, thinly sliced
- 1/2 cup mayonnaise
- 2 tablespoons Dijon mustard
- 2 tablespoons honey
- 2 tablespoons apple cider vinegar
- 1/2 teaspoon celery seed
- 2 tablespoons chopped fresh dill
- Salt and freshly ground black pepper

Instructions:
1. In a large bowl, combine the apples, red onion, and cabbage.
2. In a separate bowl, whisk together the mayonnaise, mustard, honey, vinegar, celery seed, and dill.
3. Pour the dressing over the apple mixture and stir to combine.
4. Add salt and freshly ground pepper to taste.
5. Serve chilled.

Nutrition Information per Serving:
Calories: 239, Fat: 17.5g, Carbohydrates: 20.2g, Protein: 1.3g, Sodium: 123mg, Sugar: 11.5g

13. Italian Apple Coleslaw

Italian Apple Coleslaw is a fruity twist on the traditional coleslaw. It is an easy and colorful dish that will please everyone at your table.
Serving: 6
Prep Time: 15 minutes
Ready Time: 15 minutes

Ingredients:
- 4 cups shredded cabbage
- 1 red pepper, diced
- 2 green onions, sliced
- 1 large Granny Smith apple, peeled and diced
- 1 cup mayonnaise
- 1/4 cup sugar

- 1 teaspoon celery seed
- 2 tablespoons apple cider vinegar

Instructions:
1. In a large bowl, mix together the cabbage, red pepper, green onions, and apple.
2. In a separate bowl, mix together the mayonnaise, sugar, celery seed, and apple cider vinegar.
3. Pour the dressing over the cabbage mixture and toss until everything is combined.
4. Refrigerate for at least 30 minutes before serving.

Nutrition Information per Serving:
Calories: 224 kcal, Carbohydrates: 23 g, Protein: 2 g, Fat: 16 g, Saturated Fat: 3 g, Cholesterol: 8 mg, Sodium: 271 mg, Potassium: 149 mg, Fiber: 3 g, Sugar: 18 g, Vitamin A: 567 IU, Vitamin C: 47 mg, Calcium: 39 mg, Iron: 1 mg

14. French Apple Coleslaw

French Apple Coleslaw is a tangy, deliciously crunchy side dish made with crisp apples, cabbage, and a creamy dressing made with mayonnaise, cider vinegar, and maple syrup.
Serving: Serves 6
Preparation time: 10 min
Ready time: 30 min

Ingredients:
- 2 granny smith apples, shredded
- 1 cup cabbage, shredded
- 2 tablespoons mayonnaise
- 2 tablespoons cider vinegar
- 2 tablespoons maple syrup
- 1 teaspoon mustard
- Salt and pepper to taste

Instructions:
1. In a large bowl, combine shredded apples and cabbage.

2. In a separate bowl, mix mayonnaise, cider vinegar, maple syrup, mustard, salt and pepper.
3. Pour dressing over apple and cabbage mixture and toss until evenly coating.
4. Cover and refrigerate for at least 20 minutes before serving.

Nutrition Information: Per serving: 80 calories, 4 g fat, 10 g carbohydrates, 1 g protein, 16 mg sodium.

15. Japanese Apple Coleslaw

Japanese Apple Coleslaw is a light and refreshing side dish that pairs well with any meal. It uses sweet apples and crunchy cabbage to make a flavorful coleslaw that will brighten up your dinner table.
Serving: Servings 4-6
Preparation Time: 10 minutes
Ready Time: 20 minutes

Ingredients:
- 1 head green cabbage, shredded
- 3 apples, peeled and shredded
- 1/4 cup rice vinegar
- 2 tablespoons vegetable oil
- 2 tablespoons sugar
- Salt and pepper, to taste

Instructions:
1. In a large bowl, combine cabbage and apples.
2. In a small bowl, whisk together rice vinegar, vegetable oil, sugar, salt and pepper.
3. Pour the dressing over the cabbage and apples and mix to coat.
4. Refrigerate for at least 1 hour.

Nutrition Information: 160 calories, 9 g fat, 21 g carbohydrates, 2 g protein

16. Korean Apple Coleslaw

Korean Apple Coleslaw is a unique and flavorful twist on traditional coleslaw. This recipe features green apples, kale, and red cabbage that are tossed in a tangy sweet and sour poached Korean pear dressing. It's sure to be a hit at any party or potluck!

Serving: Serves 8
Preparation Time: 15 minutes
Ready Time: 25 minutes

Ingredients:
- 1/3 head red cabbage, shredded
- 1/2 bunch kale, stemmed and leaves thinly sliced
- 2 green apples, peeled and thinly sliced
- 6 cloves garlic, minced
- 4 tablespoons white vinegar
- 1 poached Korean pear, peeled, cored, and chopped
- 2 tablespoons honey
- 3 tablespoons soy sauce
- 1/4 cup extra-virgin olive oil

Instructions:
1. In a large bowl, combine the shredded cabbage, kale, and apples.
2. In a small bowl, whisk together the garlic, vinegar, poached pear, honey, soy sauce, and olive oil.
3. Pour the dressing over the salad and toss to combine.
4. Let the salad sit for at least 10 minutes before serving.

Nutrition Information: (per serving):
Calories: 125 kcal
Fat: 8 g
Carbohydrates: 12 g
Protein: 2 g
Sodium: 258 mg
Potassium: 211 mg
Fiber: 2 g
Sugar: 8 g

17. Vietnamese Apple Coleslaw

Vietnamese Apple Coleslaw
Serving: 4
Preparation time: 20 minutes
Ready time: 20 minutes

Ingredients:
- 2 tablespoons lime juice
- 2 tablespoons fish sauce
- 2 tablespoons honey
- 2 tablespoons chopped fresh Thai chilies
- 2 golden delicious apples, cored and thinly sliced
- Half a head of red cabbage, finely shredded
- 2 carrots, julienned
- 1/2 cup cilantro leaves
- 1/4 cup unsalted roasted peanuts, coarsely chopped

Instructions:
1. In a small bowl, whisk together the lime juice, fish sauce, honey, and chilies until well combined.
2. In a large bowl, combine the apple, cabbage, carrots, and cilantro. Pour the dressing over the salad and toss to combine.
3. Sprinkle with the peanuts and serve.

Nutrition Information: Calories: 130, Total Fat: 5 g, Saturated Fat: 1 g, Cholesterol: 0 mg, Sodium: 230 mg, Carbohydrates: 18 g, Fiber: 5 g, Sugar: 11 g, Protein: 4 g

18. Chinese Apple Coleslaw

Chinese Apple Coleslaw
Serving: 4
Preparation Time: 10 minutes
Ready Time: 15 minutes

Ingredients:
- 2 cups shredded cabbage

- 1 diced apple
- 2 tablespoons honey
- Juice from 1 lemon
- 2 tablespoons olive oil
- 1/4 teaspoon salt
- Ground black pepper, to taste

Instructions:
1. In a large bowl, mix together the cabbage and apple.
2. In a smaller bowl, whisk together the honey, lemon juice, olive oil, salt, and black pepper.
3. Pour the dressing over the cabbage and apple and mix everything together until evenly coated.
4. Refrigerate for 1-2 hours before serving. Enjoy!

Nutrition Information (per serving):
Calories: 67
Fat: 4 g
Carbohydrates: 9 g
Protein: 1 g
Sodium: 178 mg

19. Moroccan Apple Coleslaw

Moroccan Apple Coleslaw
Serving: 8-10
Preparation time: 15 minutes
Ready time: 1 hour

Ingredients:
-2 tablespoons freshly squeezed orange juice
-1 tablespoon Dijon mustard
-1/4 cup mayonnaise
-1/4 cup olive oil
-2 tablespoons white wine vinegar
-1/4 teaspoon ground cumin
-1/4 teaspoon ground coriander
-1/4 teaspoon ground cinnamon

-1/4 teaspoon sea salt
-Freshly ground black pepper
-2 large red or green apples, cored and shredded
-1/2 small red onion, finely chopped
-2 carrots, shredded
-1/2 cup raisins
-2 heads green or red cabbage, finely shredded

Instructions:
1. In a large bowl, whisk together the orange juice, mustard, mayonnaise, olive oil, white wine vinegar, cumin, coriander, cinnamon, sea salt and pepper.
2. Add the apples, onion, carrots, raisins and cabbage and toss to combine.
3. Cover and refrigerate for at least 1 hour before serving.

Nutrition Information:
Per serving: Calories: 203; Total Fat: 12.7g; Saturated Fat: 1.7g; Trans Fat: 0g; Cholesterol: 4mg; Sodium: 179mg; Total Carbohydrates: 20.6g; Dietary Fiber: 4.3g; Sugars: 14.3g; Protein: 2.4g.

20. Lebanese Apple Coleslaw

Lebanese Apple Coleslaw is a delicious, light and easy to make salad that features a classic combination of apples, cabbage, and creamy dressing. It's a great addition to any meal and is a great way to get your daily dose of vegetables.
Serving: 4
Preparation Time: 10 min
Ready Time: 10 min

Ingredients:
- 2 cups shredded cabbage
- 2 apples, cored and sliced
- 1/4 cup mayonnaise
- 2 tablespoons apple cider vinegar
- 1/4 teaspoon freshly ground black pepper
- Pinch of sea salt

Instructions:
1. In a large bowl, combine the shredded cabbage and sliced apples.
2. In a small bowl, whisk together the mayonnaise, apple cider vinegar, salt and pepper.
3. Pour the dressing mixture over the cabbage and apples, and toss to combine all Ingredients.
4. Serve chilled.

Nutrition Information: Calories: 80 | Fat: 4.5g | Carbs: 10g | Fiber: 2g | Protein: 1g

21. Egyptian Apple Coleslaw

Egyptian Apple Coleslaw is a delicious, flavorful salad that combines the sweetness of apples with the crunch of red cabbage and carrots. It's a great way to enjoy a lighter option on hot days or for a side dish that will make any meal pop!

Serving:
Makes 6 servings
Preparation Time:
20 minutes
Ready Time:
20 minutes

Ingredients:
- 1 red cabbage, sliced
- 2 carrots, grated
- 2 apples, peeled and chopped
- 1 cup light mayonnaise
- 2 tablespoons honey
- 1 teaspoon apple cider vinegar
- Salt and pepper to taste

Instructions:
1. In a large bowl, combine red cabbage, carrots, and apples.
2. In a separate bowl, mix together mayonnaise, honey, and apple cider vinegar.

3. Pour the mayonnaise mixture over the cabbage mixture and mix until all vegetables are coated.
4. Season with salt and pepper to taste.
5. Serve chilled or at room temperature.

Nutrition Information:
Per Serving: Calories 190, Total Fat 10 g (Saturated 2 g, Trans 0 g), Cholesterol 0 mg, Sodium 42 mg, Total Carbohydrate 24 g (Dietary Fiber 4 g, Total Sugars 16 g, Added Sugars 0 g), Protein 2 g.

22. Israeli Apple Coleslaw

Israeli Apple Coleslaw is a unique, sweet coleslaw recipe with a delicious tang from the crunch of apples.
Serving: 6
Preparation Time: 10 mins
Ready Time: 2 hours

Ingredients:
- 3 large apples – cored, diced
- Half a head of red cabbage – finely shredded
- 2 stalks celery – diced
- 2 tablespoons finely chopped fresh parsley
- 2 tablespoons finely chopped chives
- 4 tablespoons olive oil
- 2 tablespoons white wine vinegar
- 2 tablespoons honey
- 2 tablespoons mustard
- 2 tablespoons fresh lemon juice
- Salt and pepper to taste

Instructions:
1. In a large bowl, combine the diced apples, shredded cabbage, celery, parsley, and chives.
2. In a separate bowl, whisk together the olive oil, white wine vinegar, honey, mustard, lemon juice, and salt and pepper.
3. Pour the dressing over the slaw mixture and toss until evenly coated.

4. Allow the coleslaw to chill in the refrigerator for at least 2 hours for best flavor.

Nutrition Information: Serving Size: 1/6, Calories: 188, Total Fat: 15.3g, Saturated Fat: 2.1g, Sodium: 27.6mg, Carbohydrates: 13g, Dietary Fiber: 2.8g, Sugars: 8.3g, Protein: 1.3g.

23. Irish Apple Coleslaw

Irish Apple Coleslaw
Serving: 6
Preparation time: 15 minutes
Ready time: 25 minutes

Ingredients:
- 2 apples, thinly sliced
- 1 (14-ounce) package coleslaw mix
- 2 tablespoons fresh lemon juice
- 2 tablespoons extra-virgin olive oil
- 1 tablespoon honey
- 1 teaspoon caraway seeds
- 1/4 teaspoon salt
- Pinch of freshly ground black pepper

Instructions:
1. In a large bowl, combine the apples and coleslaw mix.
2. In a separate small bowl, whisk together the lemon juice, olive oil, honey, caraway seeds, salt, and pepper.
3. Pour the dressing over the coleslaw mixture and toss to coat.
4. Refrigerate for 10 minutes.

Nutrition Information:
- Calories: 124
- Total Fat: 6 g
- Saturated Fat: 1 g
- Cholesterol: 0 mg
- Sodium: 127 mg
- Carbohydrates: 17 g

- Dietary Fiber: 4 g
- Sugar: 10 g
- Protein: 2 g

24. Scottish Apple Coleslaw

Scottish Apple Coleslaw is a crisp and flavorful combination of finely shredded apples, shredded cabbage, and mayonnaise. This classic side dish is perfect for barbecues, picnics, and all your summer entertaining.
Serving: 8
Preparation Time: 10 minutes
Ready Time: 30 minutes

Ingredients:
- 2 cups shredded red cabbage
- 1 large tart green apple, shredded
- 1/2 cup sliced celery
- 1/4 cup mayonnaise
- 2 teaspoons white sugar
- 2 teaspoons white vinegar
- 1/4 teaspoon dried thyme
- 1/4 teaspoon poppy seeds
- Salt and black pepper to taste

Instructions:
1. In a large bowl, combine the cabbage, apple, celery, mayonnaise, sugar, vinegar, thyme, and poppy seeds.
2. Season with salt and pepper to taste.
3. Toss the coleslaw until evenly mixed.
4. Refrigerate for at least 30 minutes, until chilled.

Nutrition Information: Per serving (1/8 of recipe): 140 calories; 9.9 g fat; 1.6 g saturated fat; 2.9 g carbohydrates; 2.5 g protein.

25. Welsh Apple Coleslaw

Welsh Apple Coleslaw

Serving: 8
Preparation Time: 10 minutes
Ready Time: 30 minutes

Ingredients:
- 2 cups green cabbage, shredded
- 2 cups red cabbage, shredded
- 2 apples, finely diced
- 1/4 cup mayonnaise
- 2 tablespoons sugar
- 2 tablespoons white wine vinegar
- Salt and pepper, to taste

Instructions:
1. In a large bowl, combine the cabbages, apples and mayonnaise.
2. In a small bowl, mix together the sugar, vinegar and salt and pepper.
3. Pour the dressing over the cabbage mixture, and mix until combined.
4. Let the coleslaw sit for at least half an hour in the fridge before serving.

Nutrition Information:
Calories: 140, Fat: 7 g, Carbohydrates: 19 g, Protein: 2g, Sodium: 88 mg

26. English Apple Coleslaw

English Apple Coleslaw is a tasty and healthy side dish that combines crisp apples and cabbage with a flavorful dressing.
Serving: 4-6
Preparation Time: 10 minutes
Ready Time: 10 minutes

Ingredients:
- 3 cups shredded green cabbage
- 4 Granny Smith apples, diced
- 2/3 cup mayonnaise
- 2 tablespoons apple cider vinegar
- 2 tablespoons honey
- 1 teaspoon celery seed

- 1 teaspoon salt
- 1/2 teaspoon ground black pepper

Instructions:
1. In a large bowl, mix together shredded cabbage and diced apples.
2. In a separate bowl, mix together mayonnaise, cider vinegar, honey, celery seed, salt, and pepper.
3. Pour mayonnaise mixture over cabbage mixture and stir gently.
4. Cover and chill in the refrigerator for at least 30 minutes before serving.

Nutrition Information (per serving):
Calories: 173
Total fat: 12g
Saturated fat: 2g
Cholesterol: 10mg
Sodium: 313mg
Carbohydrates: 17g
Sugar: 14g
Protein: 1g

27. Dutch Apple Coleslaw

Dutch Apple Coleslaw is a fruity twist on the traditional coleslaw that adds a hint of sweetness to the savory dish. Perfect for barbeques and picnics, it's sure to be a crowd pleaser.
Serving: 4
Preparation Time: 10 minutes
Ready Time: 10 minutes

Ingredients:
- 2 cups shredded cabbage
- 2 cups grated carrot
- 1 large apple, cored and diced
- 2 tablespoons parsley, chopped
- 2 tablespoons mayonnaise
- 2 tablespoons sugar
- 1 tablespoon apple cider vinegar

- ½ teaspoon onion powder
- Sea salt and freshly ground black pepper, to taste

Instructions:
1. In a large bowl, combine cabbage, carrot, apple and parsley and mix together.
2. In a separate bowl, whisk together mayonnaise, sugar, apple cider vinegar and onion powder until smooth.
3. Add mayonnaise mixture to the bowl with the vegetables and mix until everything is evenly coated.
4. Season with sea salt and black pepper, to taste.
5. Serve at room temperature or chilled.

Nutrition Information: Calories: 192, Total Fat: 9g, Saturated Fat: 1g, Trans Fat: 0g, Cholesterol: 9mg, Sodium: 108mg, Carbohydrates: 24g, Fiber: 3g, Sugar: 18g, Protein: 3g

28. Belgian Apple Coleslaw

Belgian Apple Coleslaw is a fantastic twist on the classic slaw recipe. This light and crunchy salad is a perfect accompaniment to a variety of meals, making it a great dish for any occasion.
Serving: 4-6
Preparation Time: 15 minutes
Ready Time: 1 hour

Ingredients:
- 2 apples, cored and thinly sliced
- 1/2 cup mayonnaise
- 2 tablespoons sour cream
- 2 tablespoons apple cider vinegar
- 1/4 cup white sugar
- 1/4 teaspoon celery seed
- 1/4 teaspoon ground mustard
- Salt and ground black pepper to taste
- 1 head cabbage, cored and thinly sliced
- 2 carrots, peeled and grated

Instructions:
1. In a small bowl, mix together the mayonnaise, sour cream, apple cider vinegar, sugar, celery seed, and ground mustard until combined. Season with salt and pepper to taste.
2. In a large bowl, toss together the apples, cabbage, and carrots until combined.
3. Drizzle the dressing over the cabbage mixture and toss to coat evenly.
4. Cover and refrigerate for at least 1 hour before serving.

Nutrition Information:
Calories: 179, Fat: 11.3g, Carbohydrates: 18.2g, Protein: 2.1g, Cholesterol: 11mg, Sodium: 129mg, Potassium: 215mg, Fiber: 2.1g, Sugar: 13.3g, Vitamin A: 24%, Vitamin C: 24%, Calcium: 4%, Iron: 4%.

29. Swedish Apple Coleslaw

Swedish Apple Coleslaw is a sweet and savory side dish, perfect for a holiday feast or everyday meal. It's made with shredded cabbage, green apples, a creamy dressing, and topped with crunchy walnuts for an added texture.
Serving: 6
Preparation Time: 15 minutes
Ready Time: 15 minutes

Ingredients:
- 2 cups of finely shredded cabbage
- 1 green apple, cored and shredded
- 2 tablespoons of mayonnaise
- 2 tablespoons of sour cream
- 1 tablespoon of white vinegar
- 1 tablespoon of granulated sugar
- 2 tablespoons of finely chopped walnuts
- Salt and ground black pepper, to taste

Instructions:
1. In a large bowl, combine the shredded cabbage and apples.
2. In a small bowl, whisk together the mayonnaise, sour cream, vinegar, and sugar. Season with salt and pepper to taste.

3. Pour the dressing over the cabbage and apples and toss together until everything is evenly coated.
4. Gently fold in the chopped walnuts and stir until everything is combined.
5. Serve immediately or transfer to an airtight container for later.

Nutrition Information:
(per serving)
Calories: 75 kcal, Carbohydrates: 6.5 g, Protein: 0.9 g, Fat: 5.2 g, Saturated Fat: 1.4 g, Cholesterol: 8 mg, Sodium: 76 mg, Potassium: 112 mg, Fiber: 1.5 g, Sugar: 4.0 g, Vitamin A: 34 IU, Vitamin C: 10 mg, Calcium: 25 mg, Iron: 0.6 mg

30. Norwegian Apple Coleslaw

Norwegian Apple Coleslaw is an easy-to-make side salad that is bursting with flavor. This dish combines the sweetness of apples and raisins with the crunch of cabbage, all mixed in a tangy-sweet dressing.
Serving: 1-2
Preparation Time: 20 minutes
Ready Time: 0 minutes

Ingredients:
- 3 cups shredded cabbage
- 1 apple, diced
- 1/4 cup raisins
- 2 tablespoons olive oil
- 1 tablespoon white wine vinegar
- 1 tablespoon sugar
- 1/4 teaspoon salt
- dash of ground nutmeg

Instructions:
1. In a large bowl, combine cabbage, apple, and raisins.
2. In a separate bowl, whisk together olive oil, vinegar, sugar, salt, and nutmeg until combined.
3. Pour dressing over cabbage mixture and toss to coat.
4. Serve immediately or keep chilled until ready to serve.

Nutrition Information (per serving): Calories: 95 kcal, Carbohydrates: 15 g, Protein: 0.9 g, Fat: 4 g, Cholesterol: 0 mg, Sodium: 95 mg, Potassium: 138 mg, Fiber: 2.6 g.

31. Danish Apple Coleslaw

Danish Apple Coleslaw is a simple yet delicious coleslaw that combines the tangy and juicy flavors of apples, the crunch of cabbage, onions and celery, and a creamy, savory dressing that will keep you coming back for more.
Serving: 4
Preparation Time: 15 minutes
Ready Time: 15 minutes

Ingredients:
- 2 small apples cored and diced
- 1 head of cabbage, finely shredded
- 1/2 cup of onions, finely diced
- 1/2 cup of celery, finely diced
- 1 cup mayonnaise
- 2 tablespoon white vinegar
- 1 tablespoon honey
- 2 teaspoon celery seed
- 1 teaspoon salt
- 1/2 teaspoon black pepper

Instructions:
1. In a large bowl combine the apples, cabbage, onions, and celery
2. In a separate bowl, whisk together mayonnaise, vinegar, honey, celery seed, salt, and pepper.
3. Pour mayonnaise mixture onto the cabbage mixture and mix until everything is evenly combined.
4. Refrigerate before serving at least 30 minutes prior to serving.

Nutrition Information:
Calories: 309, Total Fat: 27.2g, Saturated Fat: 4.2g, Total Carbohydrates: 16.8g, Dietary Fiber: 3.3g, Protein: 2.4g

32. Finnish Apple Coleslaw

Finnish Apple Coleslaw is a fresh and crunchy salad made with red apples, cabbage, and mayonnaise. Perfect as a side dish to a grilled meal or as a topping for tacos!
Serving: 4
Preparation time: 10 minutes
Ready time: 10 minutes

Ingredients:
- 2 cups of shredded red cabbage
- 2 apples (any variety), cored and chopped
- 1/4 cup mayonnaise
- 2 tablespoons white or cider vinegar
- 1 tablespoon granulated sugar
- Salt and pepper to taste

Instructions:
1. In a large bowl, mix together shredded cabbage, apples, mayonnaise, vinegar, sugar, and salt and pepper.
2. Mix everything together until it is evenly coated with the mayonnaise.
3. Serve the coleslaw immediately or chill in the refrigerator until about 30 minutes before you plan to serve it.

Nutrition Information:
Per Serving (1/4 of the recipe): Calories: 128, Fat: 9.9g, Carbs: 11g, Protein: .5g

33. Estonian Apple Coleslaw

Estonian Apple Coleslaw is a delicious and easy-to-make salad that combines apples and cabbage and is seasoned with a flavorful and tangy dressing.
Serving: 4
Preparation time: 15 minutes
Ready time: 15 minutes

Ingredients:
- 2 apples, cored and sliced
- 4 cups shredded cabbage
- 1/2 cup diced white onion
- 2/3 cup mayonnaise
- 2 tablespoons sugar
- 1 tablespoon apple cider vinegar
- 1/4 teaspoon salt

Instructions:
1. In a large bowl, combine the apples, cabbage, and onion.
2. In a small bowl, whisk together the mayonnaise, sugar, apple cider vinegar, and salt.
3. Pour the dressing over the cabbage mixture and toss to combine.
4. Refrigerate for at least 1 hour before serving.

Nutrition Information: (Per Serving)
Calories: 214 kcal | Carbohydrates: 17 g | Protein: 1.2 g | Fat: 15.8 g | Saturated Fat: 2.8 g | Trans Fat: 0 g | Cholesterol: 10 mg | Sodium: 132 mg | Potassium: 248 mg | Fiber: 3.2 g | Sugar: 11 g | Vitamin A: 58 IU | Vitamin C: 24 mg | Calcium: 33 mg | Iron: 0.4 mg

34. Latvian Apple Coleslaw

A sweet and crunchy addition to any meal, Latvian Apple Coleslaw is a delicious dish that fresh apples, cabbage, and other crunchy vegetables. This easy-to-make coleslaw brings a fun and unexpected twist to the classic dish.
Serving: 4-6
Preparation Time: 10 minutes
Ready Time: 40 minutes

Ingredients:
-2 sprigs fresh dill, chopped
-2 Granny Smith apples, cut into matchsticks
-2 Tbsp fresh lemon juice
-1 small head of green cabbage, shredded

-1 small onion, minced
-1 small carrot, grated
-1/4 cup sour cream
-2 Tbsp mayonnaise
-Salt and pepper to taste

Instructions:
1. In a large bowl, combine cabbage, onion, carrot, and apple.
2. In a separate bowl, whisk together the lemon juice, sour cream, mayonnaise, salt, and pepper.
3. Pour the dressing over the cabbage and apple mixture and toss to combine.
4. Serve the coleslaw cold, garnished with dill.

Nutrition Information:
Calories: 162
Total Fat: 8.2g
Saturated Fat: 2.5g
Cholesterol: 12mg
Sodium: 133mg
Carbohydrates: 20.6g
Fiber: 5.1g
Protein: 3.4g

35. Lithuanian Apple Coleslaw

Lithuanian Apple Coleslaw is a flavorful and delicious side dish that combines tart apples, sweet red cabbage, and crunchy walnuts. A creamy mayonnaise mixture binds everything together for a dish that is incredibly satisfying.
Serving: 4-6
Preparation Time: 10 minutes
Ready Time: 30 minutes

Ingredients:
- 2 red apples, cored and cut into thin slices
- 1 cup grated red cabbage
- ¾ cup mayonnaise

- 2 tablespoons dijon mustard
- 1 tablespoon sugar
- 2 tablespoons white vinegar
- ¾ cup walnuts, coarsely chopped

Instructions:
1. In a large bowl, combine the apples, cabbage, and walnuts.
2. In a small bowl, whisk together mayonnaise, mustard, sugar, and vinegar, then fold into the larger bowl containing the apples, cabbage, and walnuts.
3. Toss the salad together until everything is evenly coated with the mayonnaise mixture.
4. Cover and let chill for 30 minutes before serving.

Nutrition Information (Per Serving):
- Calories 197 kcal
- Fat 15.2 g
- Carbohydrates 12.9 g
- Protein 2.4 g
- Cholesterol 16.7 mg
- Sodium 127 mg
- Sugar 7.7 g

36. Polish Apple Coleslaw

Polish Apple Coleslaw is a fresh and flavorful summer side dish. It pairs crunchy apples and cabbage with sweet and savory flavors of mayonnaise, honey and mustard.
Serving: 8
Preparation time: 10 minutes
Ready time: 10 minutes

Ingredients:
- 4 cups red cabbage (shredded)
- 2 cups green cabbage (shredded)
- 2 apples, (peeled, cored and in matchsticks)
- 3 tablespoons mayonnaise
- 2 tablespoons honey

- 1 tablespoon mustard
- Salt and pepper, to taste

Instructions:
1. In a large bowl, combine red and green cabbages.
2. Add apples to the mix and stir until evenly distributed.
3. In a small bowl, combine mayonnaise, honey and mustard.
4. Pour the mayonnaise mixture into the bowl of cabbage and apples and stir until all Ingredients are well coated.
5. Refrigerate for at least 30 minutes before serving.
6. Enjoy!

Nutrition Information:
Per Serving: 342 calories; 16.9 g fat; 14.3 g carbohydrates; 3.7 g protein; 44.3 mg sodium; 7.7 g sugar.

37. Russian Apple Coleslaw

Russian Apple Coleslaw
Serving: 4-6
Preparation time: 15 minutes
Ready time: 15 minutes

Ingredients:
- 4 to 5 cups of shredded green cabbage
- 1 Granny Smith apple, cored and cut into small cubes
- 1/4 cup thinly sliced red onion
- 1/4 cup grated carrot
- 1/4 cup mayonnaise
- 2 tablespoons apple cider vinegar
- 2 tablespoons honey
- Salt and pepper to taste

Instructions:
1. In a large bowl, place the cabbage, apple, red onion and carrot.
2. In a small bowl, mix together the mayonnaise, vinegar, honey, salt and pepper to create the dressing.

3. Pour the dressing over the cabbage mixture and mix everything together until evenly coated.
4. Serve chilled or at room temperature.

Nutrition Information:
(per serving)
Calories: 155; Total Fat: 8.5g; Cholesterol: 5mg; Sodium: 191mg; Carbohydrates: 18.5g; Protein: 2.2g.

38. Ukrainian Apple Coleslaw

Ukrainian Apple Coleslaw is filled with flavorful apples and crunchy cabbage and is the perfect side dish to any meal.
Serving: 6
Preparation Time: 10 minutes
Ready Time: 25 minutes

Ingredients:
- 3 cups cabbage, shredded
- 2 apples, diced
- 2 tablespoons olive oil
- 1 teaspoon honey
- 2 tablespoons apple cider vinegar
- 1 tablespoon mustard
- ½ teaspoon salt
- ¼ teaspoon black pepper

Instructions:
1. In a large bowl, combine cabbage, apples, olive oil, honey, apple cider vinegar, mustard, salt, and pepper.
2. Mix the Ingredients until everything is evenly coated.
3. Place the bowl in the refrigerator to chill for at least 15 minutes.
4. Serve chilled and enjoy!

Nutrition Information (per serving):
Calories: 125, Total Fat: 6 g, Sodium: 206 mg, Total Carbohydrate: 16 g, Protein: 1 g.

39. Hungarian Apple Coleslaw

Hungarian Apple Coleslaw is a delicious and simple side dish with a sweet and tangy dressing. It's a great way to provide a unique flavor to a classic side!
Serving: 4
Preparation Time: 15 minutes
Ready Time: 15 minutes

Ingredients:
- 4 cups finely shredded cabbage
- 2 grated apples
- ½ cup plain yogurt
- 1 tablespoon Dijon mustard
- 1 tablespoon honey
- 1 tablespoon apple cider vinegar
- 1 teaspoon sugar
- Salt and pepper to taste

Instructions:
1. In a large bowl, combine the cabbage and grated apples.
2. In a small bowl, whisk together the yogurt, mustard, honey, vinegar, sugar, salt, and pepper.
3. Pour the dressing over the cabbage and apples, and mix everything together.
4. Serve immediately or chill until ready to serve.

Nutrition Information: Per serving: 80 calories, 3g fat, 16g carbohydrates, 3g protein, 2g fiber, 75mg sodium.

40. Romanian Apple Coleslaw

Romanian Apple Coleslaw is a twist on a classic potato salad. This version combines creamy yogurt dressing with crisp apples, shredded cabbage, and herbs for a bright and flavorful side dish.
Serving: 4-5
Preparation Time: 20 minutes

Ready Time: 20 minutes

Ingredients:
- 1 apple, diced
- 4 cups green cabbage, finely shredded
- 2 tablespoons fresh parsley, finely chopped
- ½ cup nonfat plain Greek yogurt
- 2 tablespoons apple cider vinegar
- 2 teaspoons honey
- Salt and pepper to taste

Instructions:
1. In a large bowl, mix diced apple, shredded cabbage, and chopped parsley together.
2. In a separate bowl, whisk together yogurt, vinegar, honey, salt, and pepper to make the dressing.
3. Pour dressing over the cabbage mixture and stir to combine.
4. Serve and enjoy!

Nutrition Information: Per 5 oz serving: 61 calories, 0.2 g fat, 11.3 g carbohydrates, 2.6 g protein, 2.1 g fiber, and 48 mg sodium.

41. Bulgarian Apple Coleslaw

Bulgarian Apple Coleslaw is a delicious salad that combines the sweetness of apples with the crunchiness of cabbage and the creaminess and tartness of yogurt. It's easy to make and sure to delight the whole family.
Serving: 4
Preparation Time: 10 minutes
Ready Time: 10 minutes

Ingredients:
- 4 tablespoons mayonnaise
- 1 teaspoon sugar
- 2 tablespoons diced red onion
- 1/4 cup plain yogurt
- 2 tablespoons lemon juice

- 2 apples, diced
- 4 cups shredded cabbage
- Salt and pepper to taste

Instructions:
1. In a medium-sized bowl, mix together the mayonnaise, sugar, red onion, yogurt, and lemon juice.
2. Add in the diced apple and mix until it is evenly coated.
3. Add the shredded cabbage and mix until everything is evenly distributed.
4. Add salt and pepper to taste.

Nutrition Information:
Calories: 140, Protein: 2 g, Fat: 8g, Carbohydrates: 17g, Fiber: 3g, Sodium: 130mg

42. Serbian Apple Coleslaw

Serbian Apple Coleslaw is a delicious and crunchy slaw made with a blend of fresh and tangy spices. It's perfect as a side dish or topping for your favorite meals.
SERVING: 4
PREPARATION TIME: 15 mins
READY TIME: 15 mins

Ingredients:
- 1/2 cup shredded coleslaw mix
- 1/2 cup shredded carrots
- 1 cup diced apples
- 2 tablespoons yogurt
- 2 tablespoons olive oil
- 1 teaspoon sugar
- 1 teaspoon cider vinegar
- 1 teaspoon lemon juice
- 1/2 teaspoon dry mustard
- Salt and pepper to taste

Instructions:

1. In a large bowl, combine the coleslaw mix, carrots and apples.
2. In a separate bowl, whisk together the yogurt, olive oil, sugar, vinegar, lemon juice, dry mustard, salt and pepper.
3. Pour sauce over slaw mixture and toss until everything is well coated.
4. Refrigerate for at least 15 minutes before serving.

Nutrition Information: Per Serving: Calories: 126 Total Fat 5.3g, Saturated Fat 0.8g, Cholesterol 1mg, Sodium 19mg, Potassium 78mg, Total Carbohydrates 16.9g, Dietary Fiber 2.9g, Sugars 9.8g, Protein 1.8g

43. Croatian Apple Coleslaw

Croatian Apple Coleslaw
Serving: 4
Preparation Time: 10 minutes
Ready time: 20 minutes

Ingredients:
-3 cups shredded cabbage
-1/2 cup grated carrot
-1/2 cup diced apples
-1/3 cup mayonnaise
-2 tablespoons lemon juice
-2 tablespoons sugar
-Salt and pepper to taste

Instructions:
1. In a large bowl, combine the cabbage, carrot, apples, mayonnaise, lemon juice, sugar, salt, and pepper.
2. Mix the Ingredients together until they are evenly distributed.
3. Chill for 10 minutes.
4. Serve cold.

Nutrition Information (per serving):
Calories: 190, Fat: 16g, Carbs: 12g, Protein: 1g

44. Slovenian Apple Coleslaw

Slovenian Apple Coleslaw is an easy and tangy slaw that combines the perfect balance of sweet and sour. It's a wonderful accompaniment to grilled or smoked dishes, or it can be served as a side to balance out a heavier main.
Serving: 4-6
Preparation Time: 10 minutes
Ready Time: 10 minutes

Ingredients:
- 2 tart apples, shredded
- 1/2 cup slivered almonds
- 1/2 cup mayonnaise
- 1/4 cup cider vinegar
- 2 tablespoons sugar
- 1/2 teaspoon salt
- 1/4 teaspoon garlic powder
- 1/4 teaspoon ground cloves
- 1/4 teaspoon black pepper
- 4 cups shredded cabbage

Instructions:
- In a large bowl, combine shredded apples, slivered almonds, mayonnaise, cider vinegar, sugar, salt, garlic powder, ground cloves, and black pepper.
- Add the shredded cabbage and stir to combine.
- Chill for at least 2 hours before serving.

Nutrition Information:
Calories: 179, Fat: 14g, Protein: 2 g, Carbohydrates: 13 g, Fiber: 2 g, Sugar: 8 g, Sodium: 306 mg

45. Bosnian Apple Coleslaw

Bosnian Apple Coleslaw
Serving: 4
Preparation Time: 10 minutes

Ready Time: 2 hours

Ingredients:
- 1/2 sweet onion, very thinly sliced
- 2 Apples, cored and sliced into thin wedges
- 2 cups cabbage, shredded
- 1/4 cup olive oil
- 2 tablespoons apple cider vinegar
- 2 tablespoons sugar
- 1 teaspoon salt
- 1 teaspoon ground black pepper

Instructions:
1. In a large bowl, combine the onion, apples, and cabbage.
2. In a separate bowl, whisk together the olive oil, vinegar, sugar, salt, and pepper.
3. Pour the dressing over the coleslaw mixture and use a rubber spatula to mix the Ingredients until everything is evenly coated in dressing.
4. Cover and refrigerate for at least 2 hours before serving.

Nutrition Information:
Per Serving: 128 calories; 9.8 g fat; 7.6 g carbohydrates; 2.2 g protein; 4.8 g fiber.

46. Albanian Apple Coleslaw

Albanian Apple Coleslaw
Serving: 6-8
Preparation Time: 15 minutes
Ready Time: 45 minutes

Ingredients:
- 2 tablespoons finely chopped shallots
- 1 ½ tablespoons cider vinegar
- 1 teaspoon honey
- 1 teaspoon caraway seeds
- 1 teaspoon olive oil
- ½ teaspoon Dijon mustard

- 1 ¼ cup finely shredded green cabbage
- 6 medium tart apples (like Granny Smith) peeled, cored and chopped
- 1 cup finely shredded red cabbage
- ½ cup finely chopped flat leaf parsley
- Salt and pepper to taste

Instructions:
1. In a medium bowl, combine the shallots, vinegar, honey, caraway seeds, olive oil and mustard. Mix together until well combined.
2. Add the green cabbage, apples, red cabbage, and parsley, and mix until all the Ingredients are evenly combined.
3. Taste and season with salt and pepper if desired.
4. Chill for at least 30 minutes before serving.

Nutrition Information:
Calories: 105; Fat: 3g; Sodium: 34mg; Carbohydrate: 24g; Fiber: 4g; Protein: 1g.

47. Greek-style Apple Coleslaw with Feta

This delicious Greek-style Apple Coleslaw with Feta is a fresh and light way to round out any meal. It's packed with crunchy apples and salty feta and has a Greek-inspired vinaigrette that finishes it off perfectly.
Serving: 4
Preparation Time: 10 minutes
Ready Time: 10 minutes

Ingredients:
- 2 cups shredded coleslaw mix
- 2 apples, cored and chopped
- 1/4 cup feta cheese
- 1/4 cup toasted pine nuts
- 2 tablespoons extra-virgin olive oil
- 1/4 cup apple cider vinegar
- 2 tablespoons fresh lemon juice
- 1 teaspoon Dijon mustard
- 1 clove garlic, minced
- 1 teaspoon honey

- 1/4 teaspoon dried oregano
- Salt and ground black pepper to taste

Instructions:
1. In a large bowl, combine coleslaw mix, apples, feta cheese, and pine nuts.
2. In a small bowl, whisk together olive oil, apple cider vinegar, lemon juice, Dijon mustard, garlic, honey, oregano, and salt and pepper to taste.
3. Pour dressing over coleslaw and apples and toss until everything is evenly coated.
4. Serve or chill in the refrigerator until ready to serve.

Nutrition Information:
- Calories: 202 kcal
- Carbohydrates: 17.2 g
- Protein: 3.7 g
- Fat: 14.2 g
- Fiber: 2.9 g
- Sugar: 8.8 g

48. Chicken and Apple Coleslaw

Chicken and Apple Coleslaw
Serving: 4
Preparation Time: 10 minutes
Ready Time: 20 minutes

Ingredients:
  2 cups cooked, shredded chicken
  1 cup orderred slaw
  1 cup granny smith apples, diced
  1/4 cup pecans, chopped
  1/2 cup mayonnaise
  2 tablespoons Dijon mustard
  2 tablespoons apple cider vinegar
  2 teaspoons sugar
  1/2 teaspoon salt

Instructions:

1. In a large bowl, combine the cooked chicken, slaw, apples, and pecans.
2. In a separate bowl, whisk together the mayonnaise, mustard, vinegar, sugar, and salt until combined.
3. Pour the dressing over the chicken and coleslaw mixture and mix until evenly combined.
4. Refrigerate for 10 minutes before serving.

Nutrition Information (per serving):
Calories: 332
Fat: 16.4 grams
Carbohydrates: 12.9 grams
Protein: 32.4 grams

49. Turkey and Apple Coleslaw

Turkey and Apple Coleslaw is a delicious and crunchy combination of apples, cabbage, and turkey, making it a perfect summer salad. It is easy to make and pairs well with many different entrees and sides.
Serving: 4
Preparation Time: 10 minutes
Ready Time: 10 minutes

Ingredients:
1 lb turkey breast slices
1 cup grated apples
2 cups shredded cabbage
1 cup mayonnaise
3 tablespoons white vinegar
2 tablespoons honey
2 tablespoons minced purple onion
1 teaspoon poppy seeds

Instructions:
1. Cut the turkey breast into thin strips.
2. In a large bowl, mix together the turkey strips, grated apples, and shredded cabbage.

3. In a separate bowl, mix together the mayonnaise, white vinegar, honey, minced purple onion, and poppy seeds until smooth.
4. Pour the dressing over the turkey and apple mixture and stir until everything is evenly coated in the dressing.
5. Cover the bowl and chill in the refrigerator for at least 1 hour before serving.

Nutrition Information:
Calories: 260
Fat: 13g
Carbohydrates: 13g
Protein: 19g
Fiber: 2g

50. Pork and Apple Coleslaw

Pork and Apple Coleslaw
Serving: 6-8
Preparation time: 15 minutes
Ready Time: 15 minutes

Ingredients:
- 2 cups shredded cooked pork
- 2 apples (cored and sliced)
- 2 cups shredded cabbage
- 1/4 cup mayonnaise
- 2 tablespoons apple cider vinegar
- 1/4 teaspoon salt
- 1/4 teaspoon pepper
- 2 tablespoons diced sweet onion
- 2 tablespoons chopped fresh parsley

Instructions:
1. In a large bowl, combine the pork, apples, cabbage, mayonnaise, vinegar, salt, pepper, onion, and parsley.
2. Mix until everything is evenly coated with the dressing.
3. Serve immediately or store in the refrigerator until ready to serve.

Nutrition Information:
Calories: 206 | Fat: 14g | Protein: 11g | Carbohydrates: 14g | Fiber: 2g | Sugar: 8g | Sodium: 168mg

Pork and Apple Coleslaw is a delicious and easy to make dish perfect for any occasion. This recipe is bursting with flavor, combining cooked pork, apples, cabbage, mayonnaise, vinegar, salt, pepper, onion, and fresh parsley. Making this coleslaw is simple and satisfying and perfect for a summer BBQ or weeknight dinner.

51. Beef and Apple Coleslaw

This Beef and Apple Coleslaw is a delicious and easy-to-make recipe that pairs perfectly with a juicy burger and fries. It features crunchy apples, savory slivered beef, and a creamy coleslaw dressing.

Serving: 3-4
Preparation Time: 10 minutes
Ready Time: 15 minutes

Ingredients:
- 2 cups coleslaw mix
- 1/2 cup cooked slivered beef
- 1/2 cup diced apples
- 1/4 cup mayonnaise
- 1 tablespoon apple cider vinegar
- 1 tablespoon Dijon mustard
- Salt and pepper, to taste

Instructions:
1. In a large bowl, combine the coleslaw mix, slivered beef, and diced apples.
2. In a small bowl, whisk together the mayonnaise, apple cider vinegar, Dijon mustard, salt, and pepper.
3. Pour the dressing over the coleslaw and mix well.
4. Serve the coleslaw immediately, or chill in the refrigerator for up to 3 days.

Nutrition Information:

Calories: 206 calories, Carbohydrates: 5 g, Protein: 4 g, Fat: 19 g, Saturated Fat: 3 g, Cholesterol: 6 mg, Sodium: 170 mg, Potassium: 174 mg, Fiber: 1 g, Sugar: 3 g, Vitamin A: 383 IU, Vitamin C: 5 mg, Calcium: 13 mg, Iron: 1 mg

52. Fish and Apple Coleslaw

Fish and Apple Coleslaw
This fish and apple coleslaw combines the crunchy texture of slaw and juiciness of apples to create a unique, delicious side dish. Serve it with grilled fish for the perfect summer meal.
Serving: 4
Preparation time: 15 mins
Ready time: 15 mins

Ingredients:
- 2 cups chopped fish
- 1 cup shredded coleslaw
- 1 green apple, peeled and finely chopped
- 2 tablespoons olive oil
- 2 tablespoons lemon juice
- 1 teaspoon sugar
- ½ teaspoon salt
- ¼ teaspoon pepper

Instructions:
1. In a medium bowl, combine the fish, coleslaw, and apple.
2. In a small bowl, whisk together the oil, lemon juice, sugar, salt, and pepper.
3. Pour the dressing over the fish and coleslaw, and gently toss until evenly coated.
4. Refrigerate for 15 minutes or until chilled and ready to serve.

Nutrition Information:
Calories: 190 kcal, Carbohydrates: 7g, Protein: 12g, Fat: 12g, Saturated Fat: 2g, Cholesterol: 57mg, Sodium: 285mg, Potassium: 242mg, Fiber: 2g, Sugar: 5g, Vitamin A: 452 IU, Vitamin C: 17mg, Calcium: 56mg, Iron: 1mg

53. Shrimp and Apple Coleslaw

Shrimp and Apple Coleslaw – A delightful combination of crunchy and sweet, this coleslaw recipe celebrates the marriage of shrimp and apples for an unforgettable summer side dish.
Serving: 6-8
Preparation Time: 10 minutes
Ready Time: 30 minutes

Ingredients:
- 9 ounces cooked, peeled, and deveined shrimp,
- 2 cups coleslaw mix
- 1 large Granny Smith apple, thinly sliced
- 1/4 cup thinly sliced red onion
- 1/3 cup mayonnaise
- 2 tablespoons whole-grain mustard
- 1 tablespoon white wine vinegar
- Salt and freshly ground black pepper, to taste

Instructions:
1. In a medium bowl, combine the cooked shrimp, coleslaw mix, apple, onion, mayonnaise, mustard, and vinegar.
2. Season with salt and pepper, to taste.
3. Gently mix together until evenly combined.
4. Refrigerate for about 30 minutes to allow the flavors to meld and the coleslaw to firm up.

Nutrition Information:
Calories: 248, Fat: 14.2g, Carbs: 9.3g, Protein: 18.4g

54. Crab and Apple Coleslaw

This Crab and Apple Coleslaw is an easy and delicious side dish! Made with tender crab meat, sweet apples, crunchy cabbage, and a tangy vinaigrette dressing. This is an ideal dish for barbecues, potlucks, or to serve alongside any seafood dinner.

Serving: Makes 8 servings
Preparation Time: 10 minutes
Ready Time: 10 minutes

Ingredients:
- 1 pound cooked crabmeat
- 2 cups sliced cabbage
- 2 celery stalks, thinly sliced
- 1/2 red onion, sliced
- 1/2 cup mayonnaise
- 2 tablespoons white wine vinegar
- 2 teaspoons Dijon mustard
- Salt and pepper to taste
- 1/2 cup diced apple

Instructions:
1. In a medium bowl, combine the crabmeat, cabbage, celery, and onion.
2. In a separate small bowl, whisk together the mayonnaise, vinegar, Dijon mustard, salt, and pepper.
3. Pour the dressing over the crab and vegetable mixture and toss to combine.
4. Add the diced apple to the bowl and mix until all of the Ingredients are evenly coated with the dressing.

Nutrition Information: Per serving: 110 calories, 10g fat, 1.3g carbs, 7g protein.

55. Lobster and Apple Coleslaw

This Lobster and Apple Coleslaw dish combines the naturally sweet taste of apple with the savory flavor of lobster in a creamy blend of crunchy coleslaw.
Servings: 4
Preparation Time: 10 minutes
Ready Time: 15 minutes

Ingredients:
- Bottled coleslaw dressing, or mayonnaise

- 1/2 cup of lobster meat, cooked and sliced
- 2 apples, peeled and diced
- 2 cups of coleslaw mix
- 2 tablespoons of maple syrup
- Salt and pepper, to taste

Instructions:
1. In a bowl, mix the coleslaw dressing or mayonnaise with the maple syrup and season with salt and pepper.
2. Add the diced apples, lobster meat and coleslaw mix and stir until evenly distributed.
3. Refrigerate for 15 minutes before serving.

Nutrition Information (per serving):
Calories: 188
Fat: 11g
Saturated Fat: 2g
Carbohydrates: 17g
Protein: 9g
Sodium: 229mg

56. Scallop and Apple Coleslaw

This refreshing coleslaw features sweet apples, crunchy scallops, and tangy lime juice for a unique twist on a classic side dish.
Serving: 6
Preparation Time: 10 minutes
Ready Time: 10 minutes

Ingredients:
- 1/4 cup mayonnaise
- 1/4 cup plain Greek yogurt
- 2 tablespoons lime juice
- 2 tablespoons honey
- 2 teaspoons Dijon mustard
- 1/2 teaspoon kosher salt
- 2 cups shredded red cabbage
- 1/2 cup chopped green onion

- 3/4 cup chopped unpeeled apple
- 3/4 cup cooked scallops, diced

Instructions:
1. In a small bowl whisk together mayonnaise, yogurt, lime juice, honey, mustard and salt.
2. In a large bowl combine cabbage, green onion, apple and scallops.
3. Pour the mayo mixture over the cabbage mixture and mix until combined.
4. Serve chilled or at room temperature.

Nutrition Information: Servings per recipe: 6; per serving: calories 97; fat 7 g; saturated fat 1 g; cholesterol 10 mg; sodium 138 mg; carbohydrates 7 g; fiber 1 g; sugar 5 g; protein 2 g.

57. Tuna and Apple Coleslaw

Tuna and Apple Coleslaw is a delicious combination of tuna, apples, and crunchy cabbage in a creamy dressing. Served over a bed of greens for a refreshing meal.
Serving: 6
Preparation Time: 15 minutes
Ready time: 15 minutes

Ingredients:
-2 5-ounce cans of tuna, drained
-4 cups of shredded cabbage
-2 apples, cored and diced
-1/2 cup of mayonnaise
-2 tablespoons of white wine vinegar
-1 teaspoon of salt
-1/4 teaspoon of black pepper

Instructions:
1. In a large bowl, combine the tuna, cabbage, and apples.
2. In a separate bowl, whisk together the mayonnaise, vinegar, salt, and pepper.
3. Pour the dressing over the tuna mixture and toss to combine.

4. Serve over a bed of greens.

Nutrition Information: Serving Size: 1/6 of recipe; Calories: 239; Total Fat: 16.5g; Saturated Fat: 2.6g; Cholesterol: 20mg; Sodium: 543mg; Total Carbohydrates: 15.5g; Fiber: 3.3g; Protein: 11.1g.

58. Salmon and Apple Coleslaw

This amazing combination of salmon and apple coleslaw packs a flavorful punch with its crunchy cabbage and sweet apple elements.
Servings: 6
Preparation Time: 15 minutes
Ready Time: 15 minutes

Ingredients:
- 1 ½ cups cooked, boneless, skinless salmon, flaked
- 2 cups thinly sliced cabbage
- ¼ cup thinly sliced red onion
- 1 small crisp apple, diced
- ¼ cup mayonnaise
- 1 tablespoon white vinegar
- 1 teaspoon Dijon mustard
- 2 tablespoons sugar
- ¼ teaspoon salt
- ¼ teaspoon freshly ground black pepper

Instructions:
1. In a large bowl, combine the cabbage, red onion, and apple.
2. In a small bowl, whisk together the mayonnaise, vinegar, mustard, sugar, salt, and pepper.
3. Pour the dressing mixture over the cabbage mixture and toss to coat evenly.
4. Gently fold in the salmon and mix until evenly distributed.
5. Place in the refrigerator to chill for at least 15 minutes.

Nutrition Information (per serving):
- Calories: 204 kcal
- Fat: 14.5 g

- Saturated Fat: 2.2 g
- Carbohydrates: 8.8 g
- Fiber: 2.2 g
- Protein: 10.5 g
- Sodium: 213 mg

59. Trout and Apple Coleslaw

Here is a delectable recipe for Trout and Apple Coleslaw that is easy to make and can be served as a side dish or a light summer supper.
Serving: 4
Preparation Time: 15 minutes
Ready Time: 15 minutes

Ingredients:
-1/2 cup mayonnaise or plain yogurt
-1/4 teaspoon sugar
-1/4 cup white wine vinegar
-1/4 teaspoon dry mustard
-1/4 teaspoon curry powder
-Salt and pepper to taste
-1/4 cup diced onions
-2 apples, chopped
-1/4 cup diced celery
-1/4 cup grated carrots
-1/4 cup sliced almonds
-1/2 pound cooked trout fillets, flaked
-1/4 cup chopped fresh herbs (e.g. parsley, dill, or chives)

Instructions:
1. In a medium bowl, combine mayonnaise or yogurt, sugar, vinegar, mustard, curry powder, salt and pepper. Mix well.
2. Add onions, apples, celery, carrots, almonds, trout fillets, and herbs.
3. Toss to combine.
4. Serve chilled.

Nutrition Information: Calories: 241 per serving; Fat: 17g; Cholesterol: 36 mg; Sodium: 266 mg; Carbohydrates: 14g; Fiber: 4g; Protein: 11g

60. Halibut and Apple Coleslaw

Halibut and Apple Coleslaw is a mouthwatering and light meal combining the succulent flavors of fish and the crunch of sweet apples and crunchy cabbage.
Serving: 4
Preparation Time: 10 minutes
Ready Time: 15 minutes

Ingredients:
- 2 halibut fillets
- 2 apples (Granny Smith or Honey Crisp), diced
- 1/2 head of cabbage, shredded
- 1/2 red onion, diced
- 1/4 cup Greek yogurt
- 1/4 cup of mayonnaise
- 2 tablespoons of mustard
- Pinch of salt
- 1 teaspoon of pepper

Instructions:
1. Preheat oven to 375°F.
2. Line a baking sheet with parchment paper and place halibut fillets onto it.
3. Bake halibut for 10 minutes.
4. In a large bowl combine shredded cabbage, diced apples, diced red onion, Greek yogurt, mayonnaise, mustard, salt and pepper.
5. Mix together until all Ingredients are evenly distributed.
6. Before serving, add the halibut to the top of the coleslaw and mix lightly.
7. Serve cold and enjoy!

Nutrition Information:
Calories: 250

Total Fat: 14 g
Saturated Fat: 2 g
Cholesterol: 40 mg
Sodium: 180 mg
Total Carbohydrates: 14 g
Protein: 17 g

61. Cod and Apple Coleslaw

Cod and Apple Coleslaw
Serving: 4-6
Preparation Time:15 minutes
Ready Time: 30 minutes

Ingredients:
- 2 cups of shredded cod
- 2 apples, diced
- 2 cups shredded cabbage
- ¼ cup mayonnaise
- 2 tablespoons of apple cider vinegar
- 2 teaspoons of honey
- 1 teaspoon of lemon zest
- 1 tablespoon of fresh dill, finely chopped
- Salt and pepper to taste

Instructions:
1. In a large bowl, mix together the cod, apples and cabbage.
2. In a separate bowl, whisk together the mayonnaise, apple cider vinegar, honey, lemon zest and dill.
3. Pour the dressing over the cod mixture and toss to combine.
4. Season with salt and pepper, to taste.
5. Refrigerate for at least 15 minutes before serving.

Nutrition Information:
- Calories: 253 kcal
- Fat: 14.8 g
- Carbohydrates: 16.4 g
- Protein: 16.2 g

- Sodium: 305.3 mg

62. Haddock and Apple Coleslaw

Haddock and Apple Coleslaw is an easy and delicious dish that combines the nutty flavor of haddock with the sweet and tangy crunch of apple coleslaw. The dish makes for a great lunch or light dinner.
Serving: 4
Preparation Time: 10 minutes
Ready Time: 15 minutes

Ingredients:
- 4 skinless and boneless haddock fillets
- 4 cups of shredded green cabbage
- 2 cups of shredded red cabbage
- 1 small tart apple, cored and diced
- 1 cup of diced red onion
- ¼ cup of white balsamic vinegar
- 2 tablespoons of olive oil
- 2 tablespoons of lemon juice
- Salt and pepper to taste

Instructions:
1. Preheat the oven to 350°F.
2. Place the haddock fillets on a baking sheet and season with salt and pepper. Bake for 8-10 minutes, until the fish is cooked through.
3. Meanwhile, in a large bowl, combine the green cabbage, red cabbage, apple, red onion, white balsamic vinegar, olive oil and lemon juice. Toss to combine and season with salt and pepper to taste.
4. Once the fish is cooked, flake it with a fork and add it to the coleslaw. Toss to combine.

Nutrition Information:
Calories: 265; Total Fat: 9g; Saturated Fat: 1.5g; Cholesterol: 55mg; Sodium: 116mg; Carbohydrates: 20g; Fiber: 5.4g; Sugar: 10.6g; Protein: 21g

63. Flounder and Apple Coleslaw

This flounder and apple coleslaw is a perfect side dish for your next dinner! Hearty and tangy apples and creamy coleslaw combine with crispy flounder to create a delicious side that pairs perfectly with a variety of meals.
Serving: 6-8
Preparation Time: 10 minutes
Ready Time: 30 minutes

Ingredients:
- 1½ pounds flounder fillets
- 1 cup coleslaw mix
- 2 apples, diced
- ¼ cup mayonnaise
- 3 tablespoons apple cider vinegar
- 1 tablespoon sugar
- ½ teaspoon garlic powder
- Salt and pepper, to taste

Instructions:
1. Preheat the oven to 400°F.
2. Place the flounder fillets on a baking sheet and bake for 15 minutes, or until cooked through.
3. Meanwhile, in a large bowl, combine the coleslaw mix, apples, mayonnaise, apple cider vinegar, sugar, garlic powder, salt, and pepper.
4. Once the flounder is cooked, allow it to cool before breaking into small pieces and adding to the coleslaw mixture.
5. Mix together until well combined and serve.

Nutrition Information: Calories: 186, Total Fat: 9.3g, Cholesterol: 59.6mg, Sodium: 147.1mg, Total Carbohydrates: 8.6g, Protein: 17.0g

64. Sole and Apple Coleslaw

Sole and Apple Coleslaw – This recipe is a delicious combination of a mild flakey fish, sweet apples and crunchy vegetables. Perfect for a light summer meal.

Serving: 2-4
Preparation Time: 10 minutes
Ready Time: 10 minutes

Ingredients:
- 4 cups shredded coleslaw mix
- 2 tablespoons finely chopped onion
- 8 ounces sole filets, cooked and flaked
- 2 medium apples, peeled, cored and finely chopped
- 2 tablespoons mayonnaise
- 2 tablespoons apple juice
- 2 tablespoons lemon juice
- Salt and pepper to taste

Instructions:
1. In a large bowl, combine the coleslaw mix, onion, apples and sole.
2. In a small bowl, mix together the mayonnaise, apple juice, lemon juice and salt and pepper.
3. Pour the mixture over the slaw and mix until everything is evenly coated.
4. Refrigerate for 1 hour to allow flavors to combine.

Nutrition Information:
Serving Size: ½ cup
Calories: 113 Fat: 3.9g Cholesterol: 66.5mg Sodium: 151.9mg
Carbohydrates: 7.8g Protein: 13.2g

65. Tilapia and Apple Coleslaw

Tilapia and Apple Coleslaw is a unique and delicious dish, combining the subtle sweetness of apples with the exquisite savoriness of tilapia. This flavorful and healthy salad can be enjoyed year round and is sure to please everyone at your dinner table!
Serving: 4
Preparation time: 10 minutes
Ready time: 20 minutes

Ingredients:

- 2 large tilapia fillets
- 2 cups cabbage, shredded
- 1 apple, peeled and thinly sliced
- 2 tablespoons lemon juice
- 2 tablespoons olive oil
- 1 teaspoon sugar
- ¼ teaspoon salt
- 2 tablespoons fresh cilantro, chopped

Instructions:
1. Preheat oven to 375 degrees F.
2. Place tilapia fillets on a baking sheet and bake for 15 minutes, or until cooked through.
3. Meanwhile, in a large bowl, mix together the shredded cabbage, apple slices, lemon juice, olive oil, sugar, and salt.
4. Add the cooked tilapia, breaking it into smaller pieces, and mix until everything is combined.
5. Add the fresh cilantro and mix well.
6. Transfer the salad to individual plates and serve.

Nutrition Information:
Calories: 269; Total Fat: 12g; Saturated Fat: 2g; Cholesterol: 56mg; Sodium: 144mg; Total Carbohydrates: 19g; Dietary Fiber: 3g; Sugars: 9g; Protein: 22g

66. Catfish and Apple Coleslaw

Catfish and Apple Coleslaw
Serving: 4
Preparation Time: 10 mins
Ready Time: 10 mins

Ingredients:
- 1 tsp red chilli flakes
- 2 limes, juiced
- 1 cup of mayonnaise
- 2 tsp honey
- 1 head of green cabbage, sliced thin

- 4 catfish fillets
- 1 Granny Smith apple, sliced thin
- 1/2 cup freshly chopped cilantro
- 1/2 cup diced red onion

Instructions:
1. Preheat oven to 400 degrees.
2. In a small bowl combine the red chilli flakes, lime juice, mayonnaise and honey. Mix together until combined.
3. In a large bowl, add the cabbage, apple, cilantro, and red onion.
4. Place the catfish fillets on a greased baking sheet and bake for 8-10 minutes, or until the catfish is cooked through and flaky.
5. To the large bowl add the catfish and the sauce. Toss to coat evenly.
6. Serve and enjoy.

Nutrition Information:
Calories: 350 kcal, Carbohydrates: 28 g, Protein: 24 g, Fat: 16 g, Saturated Fat: 4 g, Cholesterol: 70 mg, Sodium: 400 mg, Potassium: 602 mg, Fiber: 7 g, Sugar: 11 g, Vitamin A: 822 IU, Vitamin C: 64 mg, Calcium: 113 mg, Iron: 2 mg

67. Mahi Mahi and Apple Coleslaw

Mahi Mahi and Apple Coleslaw is a perfect sweet and savory combination of healthy and delicious Ingredients. With sweet apples, tangy mayo, and crunchy slaw, this dish is sure to please!
Serving: 4-6
Preparation Time: 25 minutes
Ready Time: 25 minutes

Ingredients:
- 2 cups Mahi Mahi, cubed
- 2 cups red cabbage, finely chopped
- 2 apples, cored and diced
- ½ cup mayonnaise
- ¼ cup white vinegar
- 2 tablespoons sugar
- Salt and pepper to taste

Instructions:
1. In a bowl, combine Mahi Mahi cubes, cabbage, and diced apples.
2. In a separate bowl, whisk together mayonnaise, vinegar, sugar, salt and pepper.
3. Pour dressing over Mahi Mahi and apple mixture and mix to combine.
4. Serve at room temperature.

Nutrition Information: Per serving (4-6 servings): 316 calories, 25.1g fat, 5.6g carbs, 15.3g protein.

68. Red Snapper and Apple Coleslaw

This delicious recipe for Red Snapper and Apple Coleslaw is sure to please the whole family. It's a unique and delicious combination of savory and sweet flavors and textures that come together perfectly!
Serving: 4
Preparation Time: 15 minutes
Ready Time: 35 minutes

Ingredients:
- 2 large red snappers, cleaned and cut into fillets
- 2 granny smith apples, julienned
- 2 cups of shredded cabbage
- 2 carrots, julienned
- 2 tablespoons of mayonnaise
- 2 tablespoons of Dijon mustard
- 2 tablespoons of apple cider vinegar
- 1 tablespoon of sugar
- 1 tablespoon of olive oil
- Salt and pepper to taste

Instructions:
1. Preheat oven to 375 degrees F.
2. Place snapper fillets onto a greased baking sheet.
3. Bake for 20 minutes or until fish is cooked through.

4. Meanwhile prepare the coleslaw by combining apples, cabbage, carrots, mayonnaise, mustard, vinegar, sugar, olive oil, salt, and pepper in a large bowl.
5. Mix thoroughly to combine.
6. Serve coleslaw and fish together.

Nutrition Information:
Serving size: 1/4 of the recipe
Calories: 211
Total fat: 11 grams
Saturated fat: 2.1 grams
Cholesterol: 42 mg
Sodium: 348 mg
Total carbs: 12.5 grams
Fiber:2.8 grams
Sugar: 7.4 grams
Protein: 14.3 grams

69. Grouper and Apple Coleslaw

Grouper and Apple Coleslaw – A delicious mix of fresh Ingredients brings together a creamy coleslaw with a new twist! This flavor packed coleslaw is perfect for a light summer meal or side dish for any occasion.
Serving: 8-10
Preparation time: 15 minutes
Ready time: 45 minutes

Ingredients:
- 2 ½ cup Mayo
- ¼ cup Fresh Lemon Juice
- 1 teaspoon Dijon Mustard
- 1 teaspoon White Wine Vinegar
- 4 cups Shredded Green Cabbage
- 2 cups Shredded Apple
- 4 ounces Chunked, Cooked Grouper
- 2 tablespoons Chopped Fresh Parsley
- 2 tablespoons Chopped Fresh Cilantro
- Salt

- Freshly Ground Black Pepper

Instructions:
1. In a large bowl, combine the mayo, lemon juice, Dijon mustard, and white wine vinegar and mix together whisking until smooth.
2. Add the shredded cabbage and chopped apples, stirring until each ingredient is evenly mixed.
3. Add the cooked grouper, parsley, and cilantro and stir with a spoon until everything is combined.
4. Add salt and freshly ground black pepper to taste, stirring the mixture until everything is mixed together
5. Cover the bowl and refrigerate for 30 minutes before serving.

Nutrition Information: per serving (1/8th of recipe): Total Calories 130, Total Fat 12 g, Sodium 115 mg, Total Carbohydrates 4 g, Protein 2 g.

70. Swordfish and Apple Coleslaw

Swordfish and Apple Coleslaw
This delicious and healthy dish pairs savory swordfish with tart apple coleslaw, with the perfect amount of crunch.
Serving: 4
Preparation Time: 10 minutes
Ready Time: 25 minutes

Ingredients:
- 2 tablespoons extra-virgin olive oil
- 1 teaspoon smoked paprika
- 2 cloves garlic, minced
- 1 teaspoon sea salt
- 2 swordfish steaks, 3/4-inch thick
- 2 tablespoons chopped fresh parsley
- 6 cups shredded cabbage
- 1 large tart apple, cored and julienned
- 2 tablespoons apple cider vinegar
- 2 tablespoons mayonnaise
- 1 teaspoon mustard

- Salt and freshly ground black pepper, to taste

Instructions:
1. Preheat oven to 375 degrees F (190 degrees C).
2. In a small bowl, whisk together olive oil, smoked paprika, garlic and sea salt.
3. Place swordfish steaks in a baking dish and brush with the olive oil mixture. Bake in preheated oven for 15 to 20 minutes, or until the fish flakes easily with a fork.
4. In a large bowl, combine cabbage, apple and parsley, and toss together.
5. In a small bowl, whisk together apple cider vinegar, mayonnaise and mustard. Pour over cabbage and apple salad and toss to combine.
6. Gently flake swordfish steaks and add to the cabbage and apple salad.
7. Taste and season with salt and pepper, if desired.

Nutrition Information:
- Calories: 365 Kcal
- Total Fat: 14g
- Saturated Fat: 2g
- Trans Fat: 0g
- Cholesterol: 67mg
- Sodium: 819mg
- Total Carbohydrates: 24g
- Dietary Fiber: 5g
- Sugars: 11g
- Protein: 33g

71. Vegetable Apple Coleslaw

Vegetable Apple Coleslaw is a flavorful mix of crisp apples, cabbage, and other crunchy vegetables lightly tossed in a creamy mayonnaise dressing.
Serving: 4-6
Preparation Time: 20 minutes
Ready Time: 20 minutes

Ingredients:
- 1/2 head of green cabbage, shredded
- 1 red apple, cored and shredded

- 1/2 red onion, thinly sliced
- 1 carrot, shredded
- 1/2 cup mayonnaise
- 2 tablespoons apple cider vinegar
- 2 tablespoons honey
- 1 teaspoon salt
- 1/2 teaspoon black pepper

Instructions:
1. In a large bowl, combine shredded cabbage, shredded apple, sliced red onion, and shredded carrot.
2. In a separate bowl, whisk together mayonnaise, apple cider vinegar, honey, salt, and pepper until combined.
3. Gently fold mayonnaise mixture into vegetables and apples until everything is coated.
4. Refrigerate for 15 minutes to chill before serving.

Nutrition Information:
Calories: 155 kcal, Carbohydrates: 10 g, Protein: 1 g, Fat: 12 g, Saturated Fat: 2 g, Cholesterol: 6 mg, Sodium: 340 mg, Potassium: 155 mg, Fiber: 2 g, Sugar: 8 g, Vitamin A: 1607 IU, Vitamin C: 13 mg, Calcium: 18 mg, Iron: 0.8 mg

72. Fruit Apple Coleslaw

Fruit Apple Coleslaw is an easy and delicious dish that combines crisp apples with tangy coleslaw and sweet-tart cranberries. It's the perfect side dish when you want to add some extra flavor, sweetness, and crunch.
Serving: 4-6
Preparation Time: 10 minutes
Ready Time: 1 hour

Ingredients:
- 2 cups coleslaw mix
- 1 Granny Smith apple, grated
- 1/2 cup dried cranberries
- 1/4 cup sugar
- 2 tablespoons apple cider vinegar

- 1/4 cup mayonnaise

Instructions:
1. In a large bowl, combine the coleslaw mix, grated apple, and dried cranberries.
2. In a separate bowl whisk together the sugar, apple cider vinegar, and mayonnaise.
3. Pour mixture over coleslaw mix and stir until combined.
4. Refrigerate for 1 hour before serving.

Nutrition Information: Calories: 185, Carbohydrates: 25g, Protein: 2g, Fat: 9g, Saturated Fat: 1g, Cholesterol: 3mg, Sodium: 115mg, Potassium: 98mg, Fiber: 3g, Sugar: 16g, Vitamin A: 48%, Vitamin C: 13%, Calcium: 28%, Iron: 2%

73. Nut and Apple Coleslaw

Nut and Apple Coleslaw
Serving: 4
Preparation time: 15 minutes
Ready time: 15 minutes

Ingredients:
- ½ cup of mayonnaise
- 2 tablespoons of honey
- 2 tablespoons of white vinegar
- 2 apples, cut into thin slices
- 2 cups of diced cabbage
- 1 cup of diced, roasted nuts
- Salt and pepper, to taste

Instructions:
1. In a large bowl, mix mayonnaise, honey, and white vinegar.
2. Add the apples, cabbage, and roasted nuts, and stir until all Ingredients are evenly combined.
3. Season the coleslaw with salt and pepper to taste.
4. Serve immediately or store in the refrigerator until ready to serve.

Nutrition Information:
Calories: 225, Fat: 17g, Carbohydrates: 14g, Protein: 4g, Sodium: 163mg

74. Seed Apple Coleslaw

Seed Apple Coleslaw is a crisp and flavorful side dish that is sure to brighten up any meal. It combines the crunchy texture of apples and cabbage with savory nuts and a creamy dressing to create a light and refreshing salad.

Serving: 4
Preparation Time: 15 minutes
Ready Time: 15 minutes

Ingredients:
-1/2 head of red cabbage, finely shredded
-2 medium-sized apples, cut into thin sticks
-4 tablespoons of sunflower seeds
-4 tablespoons of pumpkin seeds
-1/4 cup of almonds, chopped
-4 tablespoons of mayonnaise
-4 tablespoons of Greek yoghurt
-2 tablespoons of honey
-1 teaspoon of vinegar
-1/2 teaspoon of mustard powder
-Salt and black pepper to taste

Instructions:
1. Start by shredding the red cabbage finely using either a knife or a food processor.
2. Cut the apples into thin sticks and set aside.
3. In a small bowl, mix together the mayonnaise, Greek yoghurt, honey, vinegar, mustard powder, and a pinch of salt and pepper.
4. In a large bowl, combine the red cabbage, apple sticks, sunflower seeds, pumpkin seeds, and almonds.
5. Pour the mayonnaise mixture over the salad and stir until all the Ingredients are well combined.
6. Refrigerate for at least 15 minutes before serving.

Nutrition Information: Per Serving: Calories: 243kcal, Carbs: 19.2g, Protein: 6.3g, Fat: 16.8g, Saturated Fat: 2.5g, Potassium: 477mg, Fiber: 3.6g, Sugar: 10.9g, Calcium: 54mg, Iron: 1.5mg

75. Cheese Apple Coleslaw

Cheese Apple Coleslaw
Serving: 4-6
Preparation Time: 10 minutes
Ready Time: 15 minutes

Ingredients:
- 2 apples, cored and shredded
- 2 carrots, shredded
- 2 cups cabbage, shredded
- 1 red onion, minced
- 1 cup sharp Cheddar cheese, shredded
- ½ cup mayonnaise
- 2 tablespoons honey
- 2 tablespoons apple cider vinegar
- 1 teaspoon celery seed
- Salt and pepper to taste

Instructions:
1. In a large bowl, mix together the apples, carrots, cabbage, red onion, and cheese.
2. In a small bowl, whisk together the mayonnaise, honey, cider vinegar, celery seed, salt, and pepper.
3. Pour the dressing over the coleslaw mix and toss until everything is well coated.
4. Refrigerate for at least 15 minutes before serving.

Nutrition Information:
Calories: 193 kcal, Carbohydrates: 10 g, Protein: 6 g, Fat: 15 g, Saturated Fat: 3 g, Cholesterol: 14 mg, Sodium: 190 mg, Potassium: 162 mg, Fiber: 2 g, Sugar: 8 g, Vitamin A: 2663 IU, Vitamin C: 14 mg, Calcium: 103 mg, Iron: 1 mg.

76. Avocado and Apple Coleslaw

Avocado and Apple Coleslaw:
This zesty side dish is a delicious way to enjoy the fresh flavors of avocado and apple. Perfect for any type of gathering, this crunchy coleslaw pairs great with barbecues, potlucks, and more.
Serving: 6-8
Preparation Time: 15 minutes
Ready Time: 15 minutes

Ingredients:
-3 cups of shredded green cabbage
-2 cups of shredded red cabbage
-2 medium apples, thinly sliced
-1 large Hass avocado, peeled and sliced
-2 tablespoons apple cider vinegar
-2 tablespoons olive oil
-1/2 teaspoon salt
-1/4 teaspoon fresh cracked black pepper
-3 tablespoons honey

Instructions:
1. In a large bowl, combine both cabbages, apple slices, and avocado.
2. In a small bowl, mix together apple cider vinegar, olive oil, salt, pepper, and honey.
3. Pour the dressing over the cabbage, apples, and avocado and quickly toss to combine.
4. Serve immediately or store in an airtight container in the refrigerator.

Nutrition Information:
Serving Size: 1/8 of the recipe
Calories: 135
Total Fat: 7.3g
Saturated Fat: 1.1g
Total Carbohydrates: 18.1g
Protein: 1.7g

77. Egg and Apple Coleslaw

Egg and Apple Coleslaw is a delicious and healthy slaw recipe that combines cooked eggs and crisp apples with a sweet and tangy dressing. This easy-to-make coleslaw recipe comes together quickly and can be served for lunch or dinner.

Serving: 4
Preparation time: 10 minutes
Ready time: 10 minutes

Ingredients:
- 3 cups coleslaw mix
- 2 eggs, hardboiled and diced
- 1 apple, cored and chopped
- 3 tablespoons mayonnaise
- 2 tablespoons yogurt
- 1 teaspoon honey
- 1 teaspoon apple cider vinegar
- Salt and pepper, to taste

Instructions:
1. In a medium bowl, combine the coleslaw mix, diced eggs, and chopped apple.
2. In a small bowl, whisk together the mayonnaise, yogurt, honey, apple cider vinegar, and season with salt and pepper to taste.
3. Pour the dressing over the coleslaw mix and stir to combine.
4. Serve chilled.

Nutrition Information per serving: Calories 107, Total Fat 8.9g, Sodium 92.5mg, Carbohydrates 4.7g, Dietary Fiber 1.3g, Sugars 3.2g, Protein 2.4g.

78. Bacon and Apple Coleslaw

This Bacon and Apple Coleslaw is a perfect side dish for any summer gathering or meal. Bursting with flavor and crunchy texture, it's a perfect balance of sweet and salty.

Serving: 6

Preparation Time: 20 minutes
Ready Time: 20 minutes

Ingredients:
- 6 strips of bacon, cooked and crumbled
- 4 cups of shredded cabbage
- 1/2 cup of red onion, diced
- 2 Granny Smith apples, peeled, cored, and diced
- 1/2 cup of mayonnaise
- 3 tablespoon apple cider vinegar
- 2 tablespoon honey
- 1 teaspoon celery seed
- 1/2 teaspoon of Dijon mustard
- Salt and pepper, to taste

Instructions:
1. In a large bowl, combine the bacon, cabbage, onion, and apples.
2. To make the dressing, whisk together the mayonnaise, apple cider vinegar, honey, celery seed, Dijon mustard, salt, and pepper.
3. Pour the dressing over the cabbage mixture and toss to coat. Taste and adjust seasoning, if needed.
4. Serve immediately, or chill until ready to serve.

Nutrition Information: (Per Serving) Calories: 155, Total Fat: 10.6g, Saturated Fat: 3g, Cholesterol: 14.3mg, Sodium: 134.9mg, Carbohydrates: 12.3g, Dietary Fiber: 2.1g, Sugars: 9.3g, Protein: 2.6g.

79. Ham and Apple Coleslaw

Ham and Apple Coleslaw is a simple side dish that is packed with flavor! Made with just a handful of Ingredients, this creamy coleslaw is the perfect accompaniment to your favorite meal.
Serving: 4
Preparation Time: 10 minutes
Ready Time: 10 minutes

Ingredients:

- 2 cups shredded cabbage
- 2 cups shredded apples
- 1/4 cup diced onion
- 1 cup diced ham
- 1/4 cup mayonnaise
- 2 tablespoons white vinegar
- 2 tablespoons sugar
- Salt and pepper, to taste

Instructions:
1. In a large bowl, combine the cabbage, apples, onion and ham.
2. In a separate small bowl, whisk together mayonnaise, vinegar and sugar.
3. Pour the mayonnaise mixture over the cabbage mixture and stir to combine.
4. Season with salt and black pepper, to taste.
5. Refrigerate for 10-15 minutes before serving.

Nutrition Information (per serving):
Calories: 160 kcal, Carbohydrates: 9 g, Protein: 7 g, Fat: 10 g, Saturated Fat: 2 g, Cholesterol: 15 mg, Sodium: 227 mg, Potassium: 168 mg, Fiber: 2 g, Sugar: 8 g, Vitamin A: 73 IU, Vitamin C: 10 mg, Calcium: 16 mg, Iron: 0.5 mg.

80. Sausage and Apple Coleslaw

Sausage and Apple Coleslaw is a classic dish that combines savory sausage with sweet apples and crunchy coleslaw for a satisfying meal.
Serving: 4 to 6 servings
Preparation Time: 10 minutes
Ready Time: 20 minutes

Ingredients:
- 1/4 cup mayonnaise
- 2 tablespoons red wine vinegar
- 1 tablespoon Dijon mustard
- Salt and pepper to taste
- 1/4 head of red cabbage, cored and thinly sliced

- 2 apples, cored and thinly sliced
- 2 carrots, grated
- 1 small onion, thinly sliced
- 5-6 cooked sausage links, sliced into coins

Instructions:
1. In a medium bowl, whisk together the mayonnaise, vinegar, mustard, salt, and pepper.
2. Add the cabbage, apples, carrots, onion, and sausage, and toss to coat everything in the dressing.
3. Let the coleslaw rest in the refrigerator for 10 minutes to allow the flavors to combine.
4. Serve chilled.

Nutrition Information: Per serving: 535 calories, 36.5g fat, 36.4g carbohydrates, 6.4g fiber, 24.3g protein.

81. Pepperoni and Apple Coleslaw

Pepperoni and Apple Coleslaw is a unique and flavorful coleslaw dish, made with a combination of typical coleslaw Ingredients, including cabbage, creamy dressing, and crunchy pepperoni, plus the addition of apples for a hint of sweetness.
Serving: 8
Preparation Time: 20 minutes
Ready Time: 20 minutes

Ingredients:
- 4 cups shredded cabbage
- 2 cups diced apples
- 1/2 cup prepared coleslaw dressing
- 2 tablespoons mayonnaise
- 1/2 cup sliced pepperoni
- 2 tablespoons freshly chopped parsley
- Salt and pepper to taste

Instructions:
1. In a large bowl, combine cabbage, apples, and pepperoni.

2. In a separate bowl, whisk together the coleslaw dressing, mayonnaise, parsley, salt, and pepper.
3. Pour the dressing mix into the other Ingredients and mix well to combine.
4. Cover the bowl with plastic wrap and chill in the refrigerator for at least 15 minutes before serving.

Nutrition Information: Serving Size: 1, Calories: 142, Total Fat: 8g, Saturated Fat: 2g, Trans Fat: 0g, Cholesterol: 13mg, Sodium: 360mg, Total Carbohydrate: 15g, Dietary Fiber: 3g, Sugars: 10g, Protein: 4g

82. Mushroom and Apple Coleslaw

Mushroom and Apple Coleslaw is a tasty, crunchy side dish that combines the earthy flavor of mushrooms with sweet tart apples, paired with a creamy coleslaw dressing.
Serving: 6
Preparation Time: 10 minutes
Ready Time: 10 minutes

Ingredients:
- 1/2 pound mushrooms, sliced
- 2 tart apples, peeled, cored, and diced
- 3 cups cabbage, finely shredded
- 1/2 cup mayonnaise
- 1 tablespoon white wine vinegar
- 1 tablespoon honey
- 1 teaspoon garlic powder
- Salt and pepper to taste

Instructions:
1. In a bowl, mix together the mushrooms, apple, and cabbage until evenly distributed.
2. In a separate bowl, whisk together the mayonnaise, vinegar, honey, garlic powder, and salt and pepper.
3. Combine the coleslaw dressing with the mushroom mixture and season with additional salt and pepper if desired.

4. Refrigerate for at least 30 minutes before serving.

Nutrition Information: Calories: 125, Fat: 8g, Saturated Fat: 1g, Cholesterol: 5mg, Sodium: 50mg, Carbohydrates: 12g, Fiber: 2g, Sugar: 9g, Protein: 2g

83. Onion and Apple Coleslaw

Onion and Apple Coleslaw is a fresh and flavorful side dish that pairs tart apples with sweet onions and a creamy dressing.
Serving: 8
Preparation Time: 10 minutes
Ready Time: 30 minutes

Ingredients:
4 cups cabbage, shredded
2 cups apples, julienned
1/2 cup sweet onion, thinly sliced
1/4 cup mayonnaise
1/4 cup Greek yogurt
3 tablespoons honey
2 tablespoons apple cider vinegar
1/4 teaspoon salt

Instructions:
1. In a large salad bowl, combine cabbage, apples, and onion.
2. In a separate smaller bowl, whisk together the mayonnaise, Greek yogurt, honey, apple cider vinegar, and salt until combined.
3. Pour the dressing over the cabbage mixture and toss until it is evenly coated.
4. Cover and chill for at least 30 minutes before serving.

Nutrition Information:
136 calories, 7.7g fat, 14.3g carbohydrates, 2.2g protein

84. Garlic and Apple Coleslaw

This simple and delicious Garlic and Apple Coleslaw is the perfect side dish to any meal. With a zesty apple and garlic-flavored dressing, this coleslaw is filled with crisp cabbage and crunchy apples.

Serving: 4
Preparation Time: 10 minutes
Ready Time: 30 minutes

Ingredients:
- 1/2 head cabbage, shredded
- 1/2 red onion, thinly sliced
- 1 red apple, grated
- 1/2 cup mayonnaise
- 2 cloves garlic, chopped
- 2 tablespoons white wine vinegar
- 1 tablespoon sugar
- 2 tablespoons olive oil
- Salt and pepper to taste

Instructions:
1. In a large bowl, combine the cabbage, onion, and apple.
2. In a small bowl, whisk together the mayonnaise, garlic, vinegar, sugar, olive oil.
3. Pour the dressing over the cabbage mixture and toss to coat evenly.
4. Season with salt and pepper to taste.
5. Refrigerate for 30 minutes before serving.

Nutrition Information:
- Calories: 159
- Total Fat: 14 g
- Saturated Fat: 2 g
- Cholesterol: 5 mg
- Sodium: 118 mg
- Total Carbohydrate: 10 g
- Dietary Fiber: 3 g
- Sugars: 6 g
- Protein: 1 g

85. Tomato and Apple Coleslaw

Tomato and Apple Coleslaw
Serving: 4-6
Preparation Time: 10 minutes
Ready Time: 10 minutes

Ingredients:
- ½ small head of green cabbage, thinly sliced
- 2 large red tomatoes, cored and diced
- 1 large sweet apple (such as Honeycrisp), cored and diced
- 3 green onions, thinly sliced
- ½ cup mayonnaise
- 1 tablespoon apple cider vinegar
- 2 teaspoons honey
- Salt and freshly ground black pepper, to taste

Instructions:
1. In a medium bowl, combine the cabbage, tomatoes, apple, and green onions.
2. In a small bowl, whisk together the mayonnaise, apple cider vinegar, honey, salt, and black pepper.
3. Pour the dressing over the cabbage mixture and stir together until everything is completely coated.
4. Serve chilled.

Nutrition Information (per serving):
Calories: 156 kcal, Carbohydrates: 10 g, Protein: 1 g, Fat: 13 g, Saturated Fat: 2 g, Cholesterol: 4 mg, Sodium: 128 mg, Potassium: 189 mg, Fiber: 2 g, Sugar: 7 g, Vitamin A: 300 IU, Vitamin C: 14.6 mg, Calcium: 28 mg, Iron: 0.4 mg

86. Cucumber and Apple Coleslaw

Cucumber and Apple Coleslaw is a fresh and crunchy coleslaw featuring cucumber, apple, and a light dressing. Satisfying yet healthy, this flavorful dish is an excellent side dish and can easily be made into a full meal.
Serving: 6

Preparation Time: 10 minutes
Ready Time: 10 minutes

Ingredients:
- 3 cups shredded cabbage
- 1 large cucumber, chopped
- 1 large apple, cored and finely chopped
- 1/4 cup mayonnaise
- 1 tablespoon apple cider vinegar
- 1/2 teaspoon sugar
- Salt and black pepper to taste

Instructions:
1. In a large bowl, combine cabbage, cucumber, and apple.
2. In a small bowl, whisk together mayonnaise, vinegar, and sugar until smooth.
3. Pour mayonnaise mixture over cabbage mixture and stir until well combined.
4. Season to taste with salt and pepper.
5. Refrigerate for at least 1 hour before serving.

Nutrition Information:
Calories: 83 kcal, Carbohydrates: 7 g, Protein: 1 g, Fat: 7 g, Saturated Fat: 1 g, Cholesterol: 2 mg, Sodium: 42 mg, Potassium: 155 mg, Fiber: 1 g, Sugar: 5 g, Vitamin A: 83 IU, Vitamin C: 12 mg, Calcium: 17 mg, Iron: 0.5 mg

87. Carrot and Apple Coleslaw

Carrot and Apple Coleslaw is a flavorful twist on the classic coleslaw dish. This unique combination of crunchy carrots and sweet apples is perfect for a potluck dish or an easy side at a backyard BBQ.
Serving: 8-10
Preparation Time: 10 minutes
Ready Time: Reveal

Ingredients:
• 4 carrots, sliced

- 2 apples, diced
- 2 Tbsp. honey
- 2 Tbsp. lemon juice
- ½ cup mayonnaise
- 1 tsp. celery salt
- 2 Tbsp. chopped fresh parsley
- 2 Tbsp. white sugar
- Salt and pepper to taste

Instructions:
1. Combine the carrots, apples, honey, lemon juice, mayonnaise, celery salt, parsley, sugar, salt and pepper in a large bowl.
2. Toss until all Ingredients are evenly mixed.
3. Refrigerate for at least 30 minutes before serving.

Nutrition Information:
Calories- 120, Total Fat- 8g, Saturated Fat- 1.5g, Cholesterol- 5mg, Sodium- 120mg, Carbohydrate- 11g, Dietary Fiber- 2g, Protein- 1g.

88. Beet and Apple Coleslaw

This Beet and Apple Coleslaw is a delicious and easy side dish that will bring flavor to your meal, made with tart apples, crunchy cabbage, and sweet beets.
Serving: 8
Preparation Time: 10 minutes
Ready Time: 1 hour chill

Ingredients:
- 1/2 cup mayonnaise
- 1 tablespoon sherry vinegar
- 3 teaspoons sugar
- 1/2 teaspoon black pepper
- 2 apples, peeled, cored, and thinly sliced
- 2 medium beets, cooked, peeled and grated
- 2 cups green cabbage, finely cut
- 2 cups red cabbage, finely cut
- 1/2 cup onion, finely cut

Instructions:
1. In a large bowl mix together the mayonnaise, sherry vinegar, sugar, and black pepper.
2. Add the apples, beets, both cabbages, and onion and mix until everything is evenly coated.
3. Cover and chill for 1 hour before serving.

Nutrition Information:
220 calories, 17g fat, 8g carbohydrates, 2g protein, 2g fiber, 320mg sodium.

89. Parsnip and Apple Coleslaw

Parsnip and Apple Coleslaw – an incredibly flavorful and colorful salad that is light and delicious.
Serving – 8
Preparation Time – 10 minutes
Ready Time – 15 minutes

Ingredients:
- 1/2 onion, chopped
- 2 parsnips, peeled and cut into small cubes
- 2 apples, diced
- 2 tablespoons cider vinegar
- 2 tablespoons olive oil
- 2 tablespoons maple syrup
- 1 teaspoon Dijon mustard
- Salt and ground pepper, to taste
- 2 tablespoons finely chopped fresh parsley

Instructions: –
1. In a large bowl, combine onion, parsnips, and apples.
2. In a small bowl, whisk together vinegar, olive oil, maple syrup, and mustard. Pour the dressing over the vegetables and apples and toss to combine.
3. Add salt and pepper to taste and sprinkle with parsley. Serve chilled or at room temperature.

Nutrition Information –
Each serving of Parsnip and Apple Coleslaw contains approximately 82 calories, 5g of fat, 10g of carbohydrates, 2g of protein, 1g of dietary fiber, and 5mg of sodium.

90. Yam and Apple Coleslaw

Yam and Apple Coleslaw is a light and refreshing mix of cooked yams, crisp sweet apples, crunchy carrots, and creamy mayonnaise.
Serving: Makes 6-8 servings
Preparation Time: 10 minutes
Ready Time: 15 minutes

Ingredients:
- 2 medium-sized yams, peeled and cubed
- 2 apples, peeled, cored, and cubed
- 1 cup grated carrots
- 2 tablespoons mayonnaise
- 2 tablespoons honey
- 2 tablespoons vinegar
- Salt and pepper, to taste

Instructions:
1. Cook the yams in a medium-sized pot of boiling water for 8-10 minutes, until they are tender.
2. Drain the yams and add them to a medium bowl.
3. Add in the apples, carrots, mayonnaise, honey, and vinegar. Mix until everything is well combined.
4. Taste and season with salt and pepper as desired.
5. Refrigerate the coleslaw for at least 15 minutes before serving.

Nutrition Information (Per Serving): Calories 130; Total Fat 5 grams; Saturated Fat 1 gram; Cholesterol 0 milligrams; Sodium 60 milligrams; Total Carbohydrates 23 grams; Dietary Fiber 4 grams; Sugar 12 grams; Protein 2 grams.

91. Sweet Potato and Apple Coleslaw

Sweet Potato and Apple Coleslaw is a unique twist on the classic coleslaw dish, where apples and sweet potatoes give this traditional favorite an extra bit of crunch and sweetness.

Serving: 6
Preparation Time: 15 minutes
Ready Time: 15 minutes

Ingredients:
- 2 cups shredded sweet potatoes
- 1 cup shredded carrots
- 1/2 cup diced celery
- 1/2 cup diced apples
- 1/3 cup mayonnaise
- 1 tablespoon cider vinegar
- 2 tablespoons sugar
- 1 teaspoon celery seed
- Salt and pepper to taste

Instructions:
1. In a large bowl, combine the sweet potatoes, carrots, celery, and apples.
2. In a separate bowl, mix together mayonnaise, cider vinegar, sugar, celery seed, and salt and pepper.
3. Pour the mayonnaise mixture over the vegetables and stir until evenly combined.
4. Refrigerate the coleslaw for at least 10 minutes before serving.

Nutrition Information: Per Serving: Calories: 175, Fat: 11g, Saturated Fat: 1.5g, Cholesterol: 4mg, Sodium: 110mg, Carbohydrates: 19g, Fiber: 4g, Sugar: 11g, Protein: 2g

CONCLUSION

Apples in Slaw: 91 Delicious Recipes for Coleslaw Lovers is a must-have cookbook for anyone who enjoys the refreshing taste of coleslaw. The book features an extensive selection of recipes, each one bursting with flavor and unique ingredients. Whether you are a fan of traditional coleslaw or looking for something new and flavorful, this cookbook has got you covered.

One of the highlights of the cookbook is the wide variety of slaw recipes that feature apples. From sweet and tangy apple coleslaw to savory and spicy apple slaw, there is something for every palate. The recipes are easy to follow and feature simple, easy-to-find ingredients. With the help of this cookbook, even beginners can make delicious coleslaw at home.

What sets this cookbook apart is the creative use of ingredients. The recipes are not limited to the usual cabbage and carrot slaw. Instead, the author has included recipes that feature unique and unexpected ingredients such as fennel, roasted beets, and pears. This cookbook is a great way to expand your culinary horizons and try new flavors.

One of the aspects that I appreciated was the wide range of recipes from different cuisines. The cookbook features recipes from all over the world, including Asia, Europe, and South America. Whether you are in the mood for a classic American slaw or a spicy Thai coleslaw, there is a recipe for you. The diverse range of recipes ensures that you will never get bored of making coleslaw.

In addition to the recipes, the cookbook includes helpful tips on how to make the perfect coleslaw. There are tips for selecting the best ingredients, chopping vegetables, and making the perfect dressing. These tips are valuable for anyone who wants to make great coleslaw at home.

Overall, I highly recommend Apples in Slaw: 91 Delicious Recipes for Coleslaw Lovers. It is a well-written cookbook that is filled with delicious and creative recipes. The author's passion for coleslaw is evident on every page, and this enthusiasm is contagious. Whether you are a seasoned cook or just starting, this cookbook is a valuable addition to any kitchen. With its easy-to-follow recipes and helpful tips, anyone can make delicious coleslaw at home.

Printed in Great Britain
by Amazon